James Ferguson

Five years' railway cases: With acts of Parliament and of Sederunt and the Railway and Canal Commission rules

1889-1893

James Ferguson

Five years' railway cases: With acts of Parliament and of Sederunt and the Railway and Canal Commission rules
1889-1893

ISBN/EAN: 9783337153373

Printed in Europe, USA, Canada, Australia, Japan

Cover: Foto ©Andreas Hilbeck / pixelio.de

More available books at **www.hansebooks.com**

FIVE YEARS'
RAILWAY CASES

1889-1893

WITH

ACTS OF PARLIAMENT AND OF SEDERUNT

AND THE

RAILWAY AND CANAL COMMISSION RULES

BEING A SUPPLEMENT TO

RAILWAY RIGHTS AND DUTIES

BY

JAMES FERGUSON
ADVOCATE

EDINBURGH
WILLIAM GREEN & SONS
LAW PUBLISHERS
1894

PREFATORY NOTE.

The following pages are published as a supplement to *Railway Rights and Duties*, produced in January 1889. The cases have been arranged as far as possible under the same headings as those used in that book, and the Digest of Scottish Cases on other branches of Railway Law appended to it. English cases on all branches of Railway Law have, however, been included in the present Digest.

The last five years have not added much to the public statutory law affecting railways. They have seen the completion of the great work of the revision of the rates and charges authorised upon our railway system, which was contemplated by the Railway and Canal Traffic Act of 1888. In 1889-90 the inquiry by the Board of Trade provided for under sect. 24 of that Act was carried out by Lord Balfour of Burleigh and Mr. Courtenay Boyle. In the session of 1891 a Joint-committee of both Houses of Parliament considered the provisional orders embodying the classification and schedules approved by the Board of Trade in the case of nine of the leading English railway companies, and the petitions against them. In 1892 Parliament completed the confirmation of the provisional orders affecting all the railways of the United Kingdom. The new rates and charges came into force on 1st January 1893.

It may be convenient to give a reference to the Acts

confirming the provisional orders relating to the Scottish Companies. They are—

Caledonian Railway,	55 and 56 Vict. c.	57
Callander and Oban Railway,	,,	58
City of Glasgow Union,	,,	59
Glasgow and South-Western,	,,	60
Great North of Scotland,	,,	61
Highland,	,,	62
North British,	,,	63

Cc. 57, 60, and 63 are applicable to other railways associated with the Caledonian, Glasgow and South-Western, and North British respectively; and the Caledonian Act includes the Portpatrick and Wigtownshire Joint Railway.

In an Act of 1889 (App. p. 69) additional powers were given to the Board of Trade in the interests of the public safety, and returns of overtime worked beyond a number of hours to be fixed by the Board of Trade ordered. Additional powers for dealing with defaulters in regard to fares were provided. The policy faintly foreshadowed in sect. 4 of the Act of 1889 was carried much further by the Act of 1893 (App. p. 75), which empowers the Board of Trade to initiate the preparation, and the Railway Commission to enforce compliance with the conditions, of a schedule of time for the duty of the servants of any railway company, which will bring the actual hours of work within reasonable limits, regard being had to all the circumstances of the traffic and the nature of the work. The Act does not apply to servants employed in clerical work or in the company's workshops. By the Conveyance of Mails Act, 1893 (App. p. 77), provision is made for questions as to the remuneration for conveyance of mails being referred to the Railway and Canal Commission; and tramways and tramroads are placed, subject to certain conditions, substantially in the same position as railways. The work of Mr. Deas, published twenty years ago, remains the standard Scottish authority on Railway Law. My aim in 1889 and 1893 has been to present in short compass a clear statement of the law and legislation relating to traffic questions, and supply the necessary statutes and administrative documents; to restate the principles and supply fully the illustrations of the last twenty years governing questions that arise in the working of a railway; and to collect all the Scottish cases on other railway questions, with—for the last five years —a reference to the English, in a form convenient for Scottish lawyers and railway men.

I have again to express my thanks to Mr. R. Stauser M'Nair, Advocate, who has verified the references and otherwise assisted me in the preparation of this Digest.

J. F.

10 WEMYSS PLACE, EDINBURGH,
January 1894.

ABSTRACT.

	PAGE
I. TRAFFIC—RATES AND REGULATION UNDER THE RAILWAY AND TRAFFIC ACTS, ETC. :—	
A.—Cases under the Railway and Canal Traffic Acts in the Ordinary Courts,	1
B.—Cases on Appeal from the Railway and Canal Commission,	4
C.—Cases before the Railway and Canal Commission,	6
D.—Miscellaneous Cases in Ordinary Courts—	
Agreements, etc.,	13
Private Waggons, etc.,	16
Running Powers,	17
Joint-stations,	18
Production of Documents,	19
II. THE COMPANY AS CARRIERS :—	
A.—Carriage of Goods,	20
B.—Carriage of Live Stock,	21
C.—Carriage of Passengers' Luggage,	25
D.—Carriage of Passengers—	
Accidents to,	26
Damages and Diligence,	30
Detention of Trains,	31
Right to Remove,	31
Right to Detain,	32
Other Questions as to Fares, etc.,	32
III. THE COMPANY AND THE PUBLIC :—	
A.—The Company and adjoining Proprietors—	
Accommodation Works,	34
Duty to Fence,	34
Liability for Damage caused in Working,	34
Minerals in Vicinity,	35
Special Obligations,	37
B.—The Company and the General Public—	
Accidents,	39
Level Crossings, etc.,	42
Maintenance and Repair of Bridges,	43
General Conduct of Traffic,	43

		PAGE
IV.	The Company and their Servants—	
	Accidents,	46
	Questions under Truck Acts and Libel,	47
V.	The Company and the Crown—	
	Questions with Post Office,	49
VI.	The Company and Contractors for the execution of Works,	49
VII.	Statutory Powers for the taking of Lands.	51
VIII.	Deficiency in Public Burdens,	57
IX.	Statutory Compensation,	57
X.	Interference with Roads and Streets,	59
XI.	Construction and Abandonment of Works,	60
XII.	Consigned Compensation and Expenses,	61
XIII.	The Company and its Creditors,	62
XIV.	Jurisdiction and Arbitration,	64
XV.	Valuation and Taxation,	65
XVI.	Miscellaneous Cases,	67

Appendix—

Public Railway Statutes subsequent to 1888,	69
Act of Sederunt, 1st June 1889,	80
Railway and Canal Commission Rules,	82

Alphabetical List of Cases,   111

Index,   119

DIGEST OF RAILWAY CASES.

1889—1893.

Supplement to " Railway Rights and Duties."

I. TRAFFIC.

(Ferguson, pp. 9-101.)

A.—CASES UNDER THE RAILWAY AND CANAL TRAFFIC ACTS IN ORDINARY COURTS.

Rules.—*Undue preference. Acts of* 1845, *sect.* 83, 1854, *sects.* 2 *and* 3, 1873, *sect.* 6, *and* 1888, *sects.* 12 *and* 58. *It is no defence to an action for charges for the carriage of goods that the charges are objectionable on the ground of undue preference under the Act of* 1854. *Transference of action.*

In 1888 a railway company sued a firm for sums due for carriage of goods over their line. The defenders pleaded that the rates sued for were illegal, and averred that mileage rates had been conceded to other traders which were refused to the defenders, "although the goods are of the same description." Subsequently they added an averment that they had been charged higher rates than other traders for the carriage of the same class of goods over precisely the same journey. The Lord Ordinary (following *Murray*, 11 R. 205) disallowed proof of the original, but allowed proof of the amended averment. The defenders reclaimed, and moved the Court to transfer the cause to the Railway Commissioners under sect. 58 of the Act of 1888, which came into operation on 1st January 1889. The Court *adhered*, and further refused to transfer, as the defence under the Act of 1854 would be as irrelevant before the Railway Commission as in the Court of Session, and therefore the defenders could take no benefit.

(The power of the Railway Commission to award damages under the Act of 1888 was pleaded in argument, and the decision seems to have proceeded on the fact that the action was raised before that Act came into operation, while it provided that no such transfer should vary or affect the rights or liabilities of any party to such an action.)

C. R. v. *Cross,* March 14, 1889, 16 R. 584, 26 S. L. R. 447.

Rates.—Undue preference. Act of 1845, *sect.* 83. *"Same portion of the line of railway."*

A railway company charged a certain rate per mile, every incomplete mile being reckoned a mile. The sidings of two collieries joined the main line of the railway within the 12th mile from T., but one was 415 yards nearer T. than the other. It was *held* that in determining, under sect. 83, the portion of the railway used by the two collieries respectively, the incomplete mile was to be considered as a whole mile in each case. The B. colliery siding joined the down line of the railway to T. The W. colliery siding joined the up line at a point 415 yards nearer T. The W. traffic for T. was carried back by the railway company to cross-over points in the immediate vicinity of the B. siding. W. traffic was, however, invariably, and B. traffic usually, carried to a siding beyond H. station in the immediate vicinity, and there marshalled for despatch to T. Both collieries were within the same mile from T.

In an action at the instance of the B. colliery proprietors against the railway company on the ground of undue preference in the rates charged for the W. traffic, the defenders contended that their contract was to carry the traffic of each colliery to T. from the respective points where it reached their railway, and that, inasmuch as the pursuers' siding joined the railway 415 yards further from T. than the W. siding, their traffic was not carried over the same portion of the railway. *Held* that it was.

Opinion that the traffic of both collieries must be viewed as carried to T. from H. station, and therefore that it passed over the same portion of the railway.

Yeats' Trustees v. G. & S. W. R., Feb. 26, 1889,
16 R. 535, 26 S. L. R. 386.

Rates.—Undue preference. Forum. Act of 1845, *sect.* 83. *Act of* 1888.

Action by railway company for sums due for carriage of goods. Defence founded on sect. 83 of Act of 1845. Plea by pursuers that this defence was incompetent in Court of Session, and that case should be remitted to the Railway Commission. *Held* that defender's plea was relevant. Similar finding pronounced in counter action for repetition of overcharges, and said action *held* competent. (*Per* L.O. Wellwood.)

N. B. R. v. Russell, 24th Nov. 1893, 1 S. L. T. 336.

Rates.—Undue preference. Set-off of overcharges.

The Railway Commissioners had decided that a railway company was giving an undue preference to another coal company as against the R. Coal Company by charging them lower rates for the conveyance of coal to certain docks than they charged to the R. Company. The railway company sued the R. Company for the amount of charges due to them. The defendants sought to set-off in a counter-claim as overcharges amounts by which the charges paid by them under protest, prior to the decision of the Commissioners, exceeded the rates paid by other companies. *Held* they could not.

The Rhymney R. Co. v. *The Rhymney Iron Co.,*
L. R. 25 Q. B. D. 146, 59 L. J., Q. B. 414.

Excessive Charges.—Whether denial of reasonable facilities, or undue preference. Act of 1854, *sect.* 2. *Act of* 1873.

The mere refusal by a railway company to receive and forward the traffic of persons in general, except upon prepayment of charges somewhat over the authorised maximum rates, is not a denial of reasonable facilities under the Acts of 1854 and 1873, and the Railway Commissioners have no jurisdiction under these Acts to restrain a railway company from making such charges, and cannot give themselves jurisdiction by finding as a fact that the demand of prepayment of such charges is a denial of reasonable facilities, or subjecting persons or their traffic to an "undue or unreasonable prejudice or disadvantage." (The remedy of the person overcharged is by action in the ordinary Courts of Law.)

(Procedure by writ of prohibition in regard to an order of the Railway Commissioners constituted by the Act of 1873.)

The Queen v. *The Railway Commissioners and the Distington Iron Co., Limited,* March 5, 1889, L. R. 22 Q. B. D. 642, 58 L. J., Q. B. 233.

Act of 1854, *sect.* 2, *Act of* 1873.—*Facilities. Preferential dock dues. Jurisdiction. Prohibition.*

The provisions of the Act of 1854, sect. 2, are limited to the conveyance and transport of traffic on a railway or canal, and do not give jurisdiction to the Railway Commissioners, on complaint under the Act of 1873, sect. 6, to restrain a company owning two separate docks twenty miles apart, and a line of railway connected with one of such docks (and thereby constituted a railway within the Railway Companies Amendment Act, 1867), from charging preferential

dock dues to the prejudice of one shipowner using the docks not connected with the line of railway, in favour of other shipowners. (*West v. L. & N. W. R.*, L. R. 5 C. P. 622, discussed and explained.)
East and West India Dock Co. v. *Shaw, Savill, & Albion Co.*, L. R. 39 Ch. D. 524.

B.—CASES APPEALED FROM THE RAILWAY AND CANAL COMMISSION UNDER THE ACT OF 1888.

Terminal Charges.—"*Services incidental to the business of a carrier.*" *Station accommodation.* Act of 1873, sect. 15, Act of 1888, sect. 10.

The Special Act of a railway company enacted that it should be lawful for the company to demand and receive certain specified rates, tolls, and charges for the conveyance of goods and minerals, "as their maximum rate of charge for the conveyance thereof along their railway including the tolls for the use of the railway and waggons or trucks and locomotive power, and every expense incidental to such conveyance except a reasonable sum for loading, covering, and unloading, and for delivery and collection and any other services incidental to the business or duty of a carrier, where such services or any of them are or is performed by the said company, and except a reasonable sum for warehousing and wharfage or for any other extraordinary services performed by the said company (in respect of which the said company may make a reasonable extra charge)."

Held by the Court of Appeal (aff. R. and C. Com.) that the company, in addition to the maximum rates for conveyance, were entitled to make a reasonable charge—

1. For share of expenses of providing and maintaining station accommodation for dealing with merchandise traffic as carriers.
2. For share of general expenses of station (*e.g.* rates and taxes, insurance, lighting and water, stationery and stores) attributable to carriers' services.
3. For share of expenses of supervision and clerkage (salary and wages of agent, clerk, and general staff) attributable as aforesaid.
4. For shunting (locomotive power, horses, staff, and stores) attributable as aforesaid.
5. For cartage (when performed by the railway company).

Sowerby & Co. v. *G. N. R.*, January 31 and March 18, 1891, 7 R. & C. T. Ca. 156, 60 L. J., Q. B. 467.

Running Powers and Facilities.—*Construction of Special Act. Condition precedent to exercise.*

The Special Act of a railway company enacted that the T. Railway Company "may run over and use with their engines and carriages and officers and servants in charge thereof for the purpose of their passenger traffic so much of the railway of the B. Company as lies between B. junction and their station at C., together with the said station and the works and conveniences connected with the said portion of railway and station. . . . Any differences which may from time to time arise between the company and the B. Company as to the terms and conditions on which the company may exercise such running powers and the tolls or other consideration to be paid to the B. Company in respect thereof, or as to the sufficiency, extent, or cost of such sidings or the removal thereof, shall be settled by arbitration." Upon an application by the T. Company for an order enjoining the B. Company to afford facilities including running powers, it was contended that the B. Company were not entitled to run their trains from B. to C. and to use C. station till the terms and conditions of use had been agreed upon or settled by arbitration.

Held by C. A. (affirming R. and C. Com.) that it was not a condition precedent to the exercise of the running powers and facilities conferred, that certain differences should be settled by arbitration.

Taff Vale R. C. v. Barry Dock and Railways C. (No. 2), Jan. 24 and June 12, 1890, 7 R. & C. T. Ca. 52 and 68.

Undue Preference.—*Lower rates or tolls. Access to competing lines. Railway Cl. (England) Act,* 1845, *Act of* 1854, *sect.* 2, *Act of* 1888, *sects.* 17, 27, 29-55.

The fact that a trader has access to a competing route for the carriage of his goods may be taken into consideration by the Railway Commissioners or the Court in deciding whether lower tolls or rates charged to such trader, constitute an undue preference.

(*Budd's* case no longer law. *Harris* 3 C. B. (N. S.) 693, *Denaby Main* case 14 Q. B. D. 209 and 11 App. Ca. 97, and *Evershed's* case 3 App. Ca. 1029 discussed and explained.)

Pickering Phipps v. *L. & N. W. R.,* March 4, 1892, L. R. 1892, 2 Q. B. 229, 61 L. J., Q. B. 379.

Undue Preference.—*Act of* 1888, *sect.* 27.

Decision of Railway Commissioners affirmed. (*See* p. 10.)
Liverpool Corn Trade Association v. *G. W. R.,*
Aug. 8, 1892, 8 T. L. R. 783.

C.—CASES BEFORE THE RAILWAY AND CANAL COMMISSION.
Procedure at Sittings in Scotland.

The first sitting in Scotland of the Railway and Canal Commission was held at Edinburgh on 10th March 1891, in the application of the Highland Railway Company against the Great North of Scotland Railway Company. It had been canvassed whether the Commissioners would desire an opening speech according to the practice in England. Lord Trayner, who presided, indicated (as was in conformity with the course pursued as to excerpts by a Commissioner in *Macfarlane* v. *N. B. R.*, Dec. 2, 1882, 4 R. and C. T. Cases 206) that the practice in the Scottish Courts should be followed, and the case proceeded as if it were an ordinary proof in which the applicants were pursuers.

Payment for "Accommodation, Conveniences, and Facilities."
Construction of Special Act.

A Special Act provided that "the H. Co. shall at all times afford to and for the G. Co. all needful accommodations, conveniences, and facilities at the station of the H. Co. at Inverness for and in respect of all traffic destined for or arriving from the railways of the G. Co., including so far as reasonably may be required, the carrying forward of through waggons and carriages in connection with the trains of the G. Co., and convenient timing, number and speed of trains," and "the payment for the accommodation and conveniences at Inverness station provided by the H. Co. under this section shall be determined by agreement or in case of difference by arbitration." On an application to decide what payment should be made for the accommodation, conveniences, and facilities afforded at Inverness station, it was *held*:—

> (1) That the forwarding of through waggons and carriages, and the convenient timing, number, and speed of trains, were facilities for carrying on the traffic of the respective companies, but not accommodation and conveniences for which payment was stipulated.
>
> (2) That the G. Co. were not liable to pay a proportion of the annual cost of working and other annual charges, and of the interest on the capital expenditure on Inverness station.
>
> (3) That the only accommodation, convenience, or facility afforded to the G. Co. at the H. Co.'s station at Inver-

ness for which payment had to be made was the portion of the said station which was occupied by the booking-office and other offices of the G. Co. Payment in the circumstances fixed at £70 per annum.

H. R. v. G. N. S. R. March 10, 1891, 7 R. & C. T. Ca. 90.

Facilities.—Resumption of passenger traffic. Act of 1854, sects. 1, 2, 3, Act of 1888, sects. 1 and 8.

The Court has jurisdiction, under the Act of 1854, to require a railway company to resume passenger traffic on a part of its line on which it has been discontinued.

(*S. E. R. C. v. R. Comrs. and Corp. of Hastings,* 5 Q. B. D. 217, 6 Q. B. D. 586, and *Dickson* v. *G. N. R.*, 18 Q. B. D. 176, considered.)

The Winsford Local Board v. *The Cheshire Lines Committee,* Feb. 8, 1890, 24 Q. B. D. 456, 59 L. J., Q. B. 372, 7 R. & C. T. Ca. 72.

Facilities.—Continuous line of communication. Passenger traffic. Act of 1854, sect. 2, Act of 1888, sects. 7 and 14.

Two companies ran trains to A., and each had a station there. They were less than a mile apart, and connected by a line belonging to one of the companies. On complaint that no passengers were conveyed on the railway between the two stations, although there was a continuous line, the Court ordered both companies to afford facilities at A. for receiving and forwarding by the one railway all the passenger traffic arriving by the other, without unreasonable delay, and without obstruction to the public desiring to use the railways as a continuous line of communication. The Court also, under sect. 14 of the Act of 1888, ordered the two companies to make mutual arrangements for the purpose of carrying such order into effect, and further to submit to the Court a scheme for approval.

Maidstone Town Council v. *S. E. R. and L. C. & D. R. C.,* Jan. 12, 1891, 7 R. & C. T. Ca. 99.

Facilities for Merchandise Traffic.—Due and reasonable. Act of 1854, sect. 2.

On a complaint that a company did not afford due facilities for merchandise traffic at N., because they had not connected their railway with a dock near their D. station there, it appeared that

the D. station was used only for passenger traffic, and that goods
and cattle had to be taken between the port and the goods station
at E. by road, a distance of nearly one mile.

Held that in the circumstances the company had not contra-
vened the Act of 1854.

Quære, how far under that Act the Court has power to order
merchandise to be received and delivered at a passenger station.

Newry Navigation Co. v. *G. N. of I. R. C..* Nov. 10, 1889,
7 R. & C. T. Ca. 176.

Undue Preference of Towns.—*Merchandise traffic. Charges disproportionate to distance. Increased cost of working traffic owing
to heavy gradients. Act of* 1854, *sect.* 2.

Circumstances in which rates were held not to sufficiently take
into account the difference of distance in favour of one town as
compared with another.

Town Comrs. of Newry v. *G. N of I. R. C.,* Nov. 5, 1889, and
July 29, 1891, 7 R. & C. T. Ca. 184.

Undue Preference.—*Carrier. Disregarding directions as to delivery
of parcels. Act of* 1854, *sect.* 2.

A railway company accepted parcels for conveyance to a place
beyond their railway, addressed "per F. & Co." They disregarded
these words, and delivered direct to the ultimate consignees by C. &
Co., who were their agents and also carriers on their own account.

Held that this was an undue preference of C. & Co., and,
though C. & Co. may have actually made the "mistakes" in
delivery, inasmuch as they occurred before the railway company's
contract of carriage was completed, and were committed by their
agents for delivery, the company were liable.

The company charged F. & Co. rates in excess of those charged
to certain persons on "a favoured list," whose parcels were
delivered under the same circumstances by the company or their
agents. C. & Co. delivered actually at the lower rates; but as
between themselves and the company, it was understood that if
they did so in the course of their employment as agents, they
must pay the difference to the railway company.

Held that the company had given themselves and their agents an
undue preference, because as between F. & Co.'s customers and
themselves the company were delivering to the customers at lower
rates than they charged to F. & Co.

Quære, how far in a question relating to undue preference the company making the contract ought to be held liable for defaults of companies over whose lines a part of the transitus takes place, but over whom they have no control.

Ford v. L. & S. W. R., Oct. 30, 1890, 7 R. & C. T. Ca. 111, 60 L. J., Q. B. 130.

Undue Preference.—Group rates. Reasonable distances. Act of 1854, sect. 2, Act of 1888, sect. 29.

Where there is a group rate which is justified on the grounds of commercial convenience, the measure of what amount of preference amounts to an "undue" preference is different from that applicable where no such rate exists.

North Lonsdale Iron and Steel Co., Limited, v. Furness R. C., L. & N. W. R., M. R., and N. E. R., January 1891, 7 R. & C. T. Ca. 146, 60 L. J., Q. B. 419.

Undue Preference.—Necessity of lower charge for securing in the interest of the public the traffic in respect of which it is made. Act of 1854, sect. 2, Act of 1888, sects. 7 and 27.

On a complaint by an association of traders in grain and flour at Liverpool against the L. & N. W. R. Co. for undue preference, in respect of the lower rates charged by them for the carriage of these goods from Cardiff to Birmingham as compared with those charged for the carriage of them from Liverpool to Birmingham, a shorter distance, it appeared that the trade of the applicants had suffered through the competition in the Birmingham market of grain and flour from the Bristol Channel and Severn ports, but that only a very small quantity was carried by the respondents from Cardiff to Birmingham. Two other railways competed with the respondents between Cardiff and Birmingham, and the lower rate complained of had been fixed with a view to competition by the respondents with the rates charged by the railways from ports in the Severn to which grain and flour were brought by sea, and which were nearer to Birmingham than Cardiff.

Held that the facts showed an undue preference by the respondents.

Examination by Wills, J., of sect. 27 of the Act of 1888.

Opinion by Sir F. Peel that sect. 27 does not limit the Court from considering any matters which might have been considered before in deciding how far a preference is undue, and how far a competition justifies lower rates.

Liverpool Corn Trade Association v. *L. & N. W. R.*, Oct. 29, 1890, L. R. 1891, 1 Q. B. 120, 60 L. J., Q. B. 76, 7 R. & C. T. Ca. 125.

With the preceding case there must be compared the decision of the Commission in the subsequent application of the same association against the Great Western Railway Company, not yet reported in the ordinary reports. The judgment of Mr. Justice Wills is, however, given at length in the *Railway News* of 7th May 1892.

The Liverpool Corn Trade Association sought redress against undue preference given by the Great Western to traffic from the Severn ports as against traffic from Birkenhead. The application was refused on the grounds that, while there was a *prima facie* case of undue preference, it appeared—

1. That the Liverpool traders were able to effectively compete in the Midland markets.
2. That the Severn ports rates had been fixed with reference to water competition between the same termini, and without intention to operate undue preference.
3. That without them the respondents would lose the Severn traffic; and
4. That the existing inequality must be maintained if the Midlands were to have the benefit of both sources of supply.

(*The Liverpool Corn Trade Association* v. *L. & N. W. R.*, L. R. 1891, 1 Q. B. 120, and *Pickering Phipps* v. *L. & N. W. R.*, L. R. 1892, 2 Q. B. 229, considered and commented on.)

The Liverpool Corn Trade Association v. *G. W. R.*, 2nd May 1892. Decision aff. on app., Aug. 8, 1892, 8 T. L. R. 783.

Order to divide Rate in Rate-book.—*Person interested.* *Act of* 1873, sect. 14, *Act of* 1888, sects. 14, 33, 34. *Power where railway company books to stations not on its own line.*

Summons dismissed on ground of imperfect information.

Opinion that the expression "person interested" in sect. 14 of the Act of 1873 is not limited to persons paying the rates which are the subject of application.

Opinion (per Wills, J., and Mr. Price) that the expression in-

TRAFFIC

cludes any person who makes out by proper evidence that the rates which he seeks to have distinguished are really and truly competitive rates with his own; (*per* Sir F. Peel) that it includes "all persons who have a *bonâ fide* interest in knowing how the particular rates which are the subject of their application are made up."

Opinion that the Court has power under the section to require a railway company to distinguish rates in its rate-books in cases in which the company books traffic to stations which are not upon its own line.

Pelsall Coal and Iron Co., Lim., v. L. & N. W. R. Co., March 14, 1889, L. R. 23 Q. B. D. 536, 7 R. & C. T. Ca. 1.

Order to distinguish in Rate-book.—Station. Act of 1873, *sect.* 14, *Act of* 1888, *sect.* 34.

In an application for an order for dissection of rates charged by a railway company to colliery owners from their own sidings or junctions with their own collieries, it appeared that the railway company kept books of the rates charged from such sidings or junctions at the nearest stations, in accordance with the provisions of sect. 34 of the Act of 1888.

Held that the powers of dissection contained in sect. 14 of the Act of 1873 did not apply to such sidings or junctions, and that the Court had no jurisdiction under sect. 34 of the Act of 1888 to order dissection of rates kept in accordance with the provisions of that section.

Pelsall Coal and Iron Co. (No. 2) v. L. & N. W. R., January 12, 1891, 7 R. & C. T. Ca. 36.

Order to distinguish Rates in Rate-book.—Person interested. Branch railway. Rates under an agreement. Costs. Act of 1873, *sect.* 14, *Act of* 1888, *sect.* 34.

On an application by the owner of a branch railway, under sect. 14 of the Act of 1873, to have the rates divided on all the traffic either taken in or given out by the applicant at the junction between the railway company's line and the applicant's branch railway.

Held that the applicant was entitled to an order in respect of the traffic inwards and in respect of all the traffic outwards, the rates for which are paid to the company by the consignor or consignee

thereof, the railway company availing themselves of the applicant's
services, and allowing for them 9d. per ton and the cartage rate.
Held further (Sir F. Peel diss.) that the applicant was not
entitled to an order in respect of the traffic outwards which she
collects on her own account as a carrier, and as to which she contracts directly with the public, from whom she receives full payment for the whole service, deducting therefrom the cartage rate
and 9d. per ton as her own proportion, and handing over the
balance to the railway company for the conveyance upon their line.
Applicant having asked too much, order made without costs.

Tomlinson v. *L. & N. W. R.*, April 16, 1890, 7 R. & C. T. Ca. 22,
63 L. T. 86.

*Construction of Special Act.—Bonus payable in respect of certain
traffic. Successful applicant ordered to pay half of defendants'
costs, as responsible for undue protraction of inquiry.*

Taff Vale R. C. v. *Barry Dock and Railways Co.* (*No.* 1), Jan. 21,
1890, 7 R. & C. T. Ca. 41.

*Branch Railway or Siding.—Severing connection with main line.
Act of 1845 (E.), sect. 76, Act of 1888, sect. 9.*

Railway company ordered at their own expense forthwith to
restore the communication between an applicant's branch railway or
siding and their line of railway, they being found to have wrongfully taken up and removed the rails forming the connection of said
branch railway or siding with their main line.

Portway v. *Colne Valley and Halstead R. C.*, 2nd June 1891,
7 R. & C. T. Ca. 102.

*Carriage and Charge for Haulage.—Haulage of new waggons sent
from manufacturer to customer. Description of traffic. Whole
or partial loading. Railways Clauses Act (England), 1845,
sects. 3, 86, and 92, M. R. Co.'s Special Act, 1846 (9 & 10
Vict. c. 326, sects. 59, 60, and 63).*

Newly-built waggons sent by the manufacturers from their
building-yard over the lines of the M. R. Co.'s system, for delivery
at their customers' works or collieries, are not, if wholly or partially
loaded, a description of traffic for which the company can under
their Act of 1846 make a charge for haulage. Nor does the circumstance that the goods carried are the property of third parties,
and admittedly loaded as a device or expedient to escape the charge

for haulage of empty waggons, entitle the company to a double charge—namely, one charge for the carriage of the goods, and another for the haulage of the waggons.

Harrison & Camm v. M. R., Dec. 19, 1892, 62 L. J., Q. B. 225.

D.—MISCELLANEOUS CASES IN ORDINARY COURTS.

Rates.—Undue preference. Agreement. "*Most favoured trader*" *clause. Repetition of overcharges.*

A railway company entered into an agreement with an iron company to carry the whole mineral and other traffic which the iron company might send, of the description and at the rates and charges specified in the third article of the agreement. In that article the traffic was divided into two classes, of which Class A included "pig-iron, coke, hewing stone, bricks, and tiles," and Class B included "rubble stone, iron-ore, coal," etc. The railway company further undertook not to carry traffic for any other trader at lower proportionate rates than those charged to the iron company, and to place the latter on the same footing as that enjoyed by the most favoured traders on the line.

Held on a construction of this agreement: (1) that it imposed an obligation on the railway company not to carry traffic inwards or outwards for any other traders at lower proportionate rates per ton per mile than those charged to the iron company, irrespective of the terminus from or to which the traffic was carried; (2) that in the case of lower rates being charged to other traders, *e.g.* for pig-iron, the iron company was entitled to a reduction only on pig-iron, and not on the other specific kinds of traffic comprised in the general class to which pig-iron belonged.

The pursuers were held not barred from repetition, it being ascertained that though their manager and their secretary had had some information of the rates charged to other traders, this information was not present to their mind when the overcharges were paid, and was not of such a character that it ought to have been present; while the defenders must be held to have known that they were violating their own agreement.

Dalmellington Iron Co. v. G. & S. W. R., Feb. 26, 1889, 16 R. 523. 26 S. L. R. 373.

Rates.—Undue preference. Agreement. "*Lower rates.*"

A railway company agreed with a coalmaster to carry his coals to Ayr at the following lump rates :—from A. (two miles) at 6d. per ton ; from B. (six miles), from C. (seven miles), and from D. (eight miles) at 8d. per ton ; and that in the event of the railway company carrying coals to Ayr for any other coalmaster at lower rates, it should be bound to reduce the rates under the agreement to those lower rates.

In an action raised by the coalmaster for repayment of alleged overcharges, he averred that the company had been carrying coals to Ayr from the L. colliery, twenty-three miles distant, for 1s. 7d. per ton, being a rate under 1d. per ton per mile, while the pursuer had been paying, in terms of the agreement, on coals carried from the D. pit to Ayr, 1d. per mile, and from the B. and C. pits a higher rate per mile.

Held that the rates fixed by the agreement were lump rates, not based on considerations of mileage alone, but graduated according to distance, a higher rate per mile being charged for short distances than for long distances, and that therefore it did not appear from the pursuers' statement that the rates charged against the L. colliery for carriage for twenty-three miles were lower rates than those charged against the pursuers for short distances, and action *dismissed* as irrelevant.

(*Mackinnon* v. *G. & S. W. R.*, 12 R. 1309, aff. 13 R. (H. L.) 89, distinguished.)

Taylor & Co. v. *G. & S. W. R.*, July 3, 1891, 18 R. 1031, 28 S. L. R. 795.

Rates.—Running powers.—Construction of contract between company and trader.

Contract and circumstances in which *held*—

1. That "route" included stations to which company booked, and carried either on own line or under running powers.
2. That "traders" was not limited to those engaged in the same line of business, but included all getting terms for same class of goods for same journey.
3. That "rates in force and from time to time exacted" described rates which, though never actually paid, were the lowest for which the Company was prepared to undertake the journey.

N. B. R. v. *Garroway*, 1 S. L. T. 224 (*per* L. O.).

Receipts.—Alternative routes. Agreement to divide. Specific and general reference.

The railway route from Inverness to Aberdeen belongs partly to the Highland and partly to the Great North of Scotland Company. For a portion of the distance from Elgin to Keith there were in 1886 two alternative routes, that *viâ* Mulben belonging to the Highland Company, and that *viâ* Craigellachie, somewhat longer, belonging to the Great North Company.

In 1886 the companies entered into a general agreement, of which one condition was that the "receipts from traffic passing over these two routes should be divided into two moieties, of which one moiety shall be deemed to be receipts in respect of traffic which has been carried *viâ* the Highland route, and the other moiety shall be deemed to be receipts in respect of traffic which has been carried *viâ* the Great North route, and such moieties shall be divided between the two companies respectively in accordance with the decision of" a named arbiter, B.

The agreement also contained a general clause of reference of "any difference arising from time to time" to G.

B. determined that the receipts were to be divided between the two companies "in accordance with their respective mileage, and under the rules of the Clearing-house."

The companies differed as to the carrying out of this award as regarded passenger traffic. The Highland Company maintained that the division was to be according to local fares, the Great North that it was to be according to mileage. The Highland appealed to G., the general arbiter. The Great North went into the reference under protest. G. determined that B.'s award "will be carried out by giving to each company their mileage proportion, not exceeding in the case of passenger traffic the local passenger fares." The companies again differed, the Highland Company maintaining that the award "meant and could only mean" that "each moiety was to be divided between the pursuers and defenders in proportion to the local fares charged by them in the case of passenger traffic actually carried by the route to which the moiety is attributed." The Great North maintained that "the true meaning of G.'s award was that the receipts are to be divided into two moieties, that one of those moieties is to be divided according to the respective mileage proportions of the two companies by the Great North route, and the other is to be divided according to the respective mileage proportions of the two companies by the other route, and that the limitation 'not exceeding the local fare' is to be read as applicable to the aggregate sum received by each company, the local fare alluded to being the local fare of the particular company for traffic by its route." They averred that "any other interpretation must ignore the division by mileage proportion, and is unwarrantable."

The Highland Company brought an action of declarator that the Great North were bound to carry out G.'s award, and that by requesting the Railway Clearing-house to divide the passenger receipts in accordance with the local fares. It was *held* that the action was irrelevant, the L. J. C., Lord Young, and Lord Lee holding that G. had no power to determine in matters which were referred to B., and Lord Rutherfurd-Clark holding that the terms of G.'s award did not support their demand.

H. R. v. G. N. S. R., July 18, 1890, 17 R. 1256, 27 S. L. R. 928.

Joint Traffic Agreement.—*Money payable at time dependent on a future contingent event. Effect of dispute as to whether certain traffic included, and of delay in verification of accounts caused by pressure of business in office. Claim for interest.*

L. C. & D. R. C. v. S. E. R. C., L. R. 1892, 1 Ch. 120.

"Dealing" with Coal.

The conveyance of coal by a railway company for use in their line, from various collieries to places within a borough on the line where it was wanted for consumption, held a "dealing" with coal within the meaning of a provisional order under the Local Government Supplemental Act, 1863, which rendered the company liable to pay tonnage rates.

N. E. R. v. Kingston-upon-Hull, 55 J. P. 309, 518, 7 T. L. R. 302.

PRIVATE WAGGONS, ETC. (Ferguson, p. 87.)

Haulage Contract.— Liability for loss of trader's waggons.

A railway company conveyed a trader's waggons containing coal along their lines, and after delivery of the coal conveyed the empty waggons back to the collieries, the sole charge made being a rate of 1s. 7½d. per ton, whereas the rate for the conveyance of coal on waggons belonging to the company was 2s. On the return journey some of the waggons were destroyed through an accident to the train caused by a latent defect in the waggon of another trader which was in the same train.

Held that the railway company were not liable for the safe delivery of the waggons as under a contract of carriage.

Question, whether the railway company would have been liable for the safe conveyance and delivery of the coal as under a contract of carriage. (*Watson* v. *N. B. R.*, 3 R. 637, approved.)

Barr & Sons v. *C. R.*, Nov. 21, 1890, 18 R. 139, 28 S. L. R. 122. Cf. article "Carriage and Conveyance" in the *Journal of Jurisprudence*, vol. xxxv., p. 618, December 1891.

Waggons property of Third Party.—Right to detain and sell for tolls.

Waggons the property of a waggon company, in which coal belonging to other coalowners is conveyed, cannot be detained and sold for default of payment of tolls due in respect of the coals. *M. S. & L. R. C.* v. *North Central Waggon Co.*, L. R. 13, App. Ca. 554, 58 L. J. Ch. 219 (aff. by C. A., L. R. 35 Ch. D. 191). (Cf. Ferguson, p. 86.)

Conveyance of Private Engine.

An engine, sent under its own steam over the line of a railway company, broke down owing to a bolt giving way. The railway company required plaintiff, the owner, to repair or to pay increased charge for transmission on a truck. He refused, maintaining that the defendants were bound to carry or convey the engine to destination, and sued for recovery of the engine and damages for its detention. Judgment giving plaintiff delivery and £15 damages reversed on appeal.

Johnson v. *N. E. R. C.*, Nov. 4, 1888, 5 *Times* L. R. 68.

As to liability for accident caused by defect in waggon of railway company supplied to colliery for loading there, while in hands of servants of colliery proprietor, see

Robinson v. *John Watson, Lim.*, Nov. 30, 1892, 20 R. 144. 30 S. L. R. 144.

RUNNING POWERS. (Ferguson, pp. 94-98.)

See—

Aberdeen Joint-station Committee, etc., p. 19.
N. B. R. v. *Garroway*, p. 14.
Taff Vale R. C., p. 5.
Sadler, p. 42.

JOINT-STATIONS. (Ferguson, pp. 98-100.)
Joint-station. Joint-committee. Joint-owner. Title to sue.

In 1864, the Scottish North-Eastern and Great North of Scotland Companies constructed a joint passenger station at Aberdeen, under the provisions of a Private Act, which declared it to be their joint property, and vested its maintenance, management, and control in a Joint-committee of six persons, three to be elected by each of the two companies, which was constituted under the Act.

The Scottish North-Eastern Company was in 1866 amalgamated with the Caledonian, and the Act of Amalgamation conferred certain rights, including running powers over the Scottish North-Eastern lines, upon the North British Company. The running power clauses authorised the North British Company to "run over and use . . . the Scottish North-Eastern lines or any part thereof, and the stations, watering-places, works, and conveniences upon and connected with the Scottish North-Eastern lines," and declared them entitled to "the conveniences and privileges after mentioned (that is to say) . . . (4) the joint or separate use of the offices, warehouses, stations, sidings, and other accommodation at the several stations, wharfs, stopping, loading and unloading places, sidings, and junctions of the Scottish North-Eastern lines, including, in so far as the (Caledonian) Company lawfully may, the station at Aberdeen and all conveniences therewith connected."

The North British Company for some years used the joint-station at Aberdeen—under protest, it was averred, and reservation of rights.

An action was raised by the Joint-committee of the station, and the Great North of Scotland Company, who were not parties to the proceedings of 1866, for declarator that the North British Company had no right without the consent of the Great North of Scotland Company to use the station, and for interdict. The defenders pleaded no title to sue, and the Lord Ordinary (Kinnear) found that pursuers were not entitled to insist in the action unless either they obtained the concurrence of the Caledonian Company as pursuers or called them as defenders. It was *held* (by the First Division, *diss.* Lord M'Laren) that the pursuers had a title to sue, and that it was not necessary to call the Caledonian Company as defenders, the North British being the assignee of their right.

Aberdeen Joint Passenger Station Committee and G. N. S. R. v.
N. B. R., June 19, 1890, 17 R. 975, 27 S. L. R. 1004.

Joint-station.—Right of third company to use under running powers.

The facility clauses and running power clauses in the Caledonian and Scottish North-Eastern Companies Amalgamation Act of 1866, giving certain rights and privileges, including those above quoted, to the North British Company in respect of Scottish East Coast traffic, were introduced by a clause which, after referring to the lines of the North British and other southern companies as forming, in connection with the Scottish North-Eastern lines, competing lines between the Metropolis and the North of Scotland, proceeded thus: "and it is expedient that the free and expeditious transit of traffic of every description should be secured and maintained over the said several lines of communication and that nothing should be done to impede or obstruct but that every reasonable facility should be afforded for promoting the free passage and transmission of such traffic," and defined the traffic in respect of which the facilities and running powers contained in the subsequent sections were granted.

It was *held* by the Court of Session that the object of the Legislature in all these clauses having been to give every possible facility for the passage of Scottish East Coast traffic upon the lines in question, the North British Company were entitled not only to running powers through the station at Aberdeen, but also to the use of the station itself, and all the conveniences and privileges connected therewith, in so far as these were enjoyed by the Caledonian Company.

This judgment was *reversed* by the House of Lords, on the ground that the rights of the Great North Company were unaffected by the Parliamentary agreement between the Caledonian and North British, to which they were not a party, and that the grammatical and natural construction of the words "including in so far as the company lawfully may" was "in so far as the company has the legal right to include" the station in question.

Aberdeen Joint-station Committee, etc., v. *N. B. R.*, May 28, 1891, 18 R. 855, 28 S. L. R. 662. In H. L., Nov. 14, 1893, 1 S. L. T. 310.

PRODUCTION OF DOCUMENTS.

Traffic Disputes.—Proof. Diligence. Railway companies havers, and not parties to action, objecting to production of documents. Prejudice.

A firm of chemical manufacturers entered into an agreement with a railway company that the whole of their traffic should be conveyed by the routes of the company, "at the rates in force from time to time and exacted from traders, whether under contract or otherwise ... all such rates not being higher than the rates in force ... by any competing railway route."

In an action by the railway company against the firm for a balance alleged to be due for the carriage of goods, the defenders averred that the pursuers had in breach of the agreement charged rates higher than those exacted by them or by two competing railway companies from nine traders whom they specified, and obtained a diligence to recover *inter alia* the rates-books, exceptional rates-books, invoice-books, day-books, or other books of the competing companies, that excerpts might be taken of all entries relating to the traffic of the specified traders and the rates charged therefor, and all accounts and invoices sent to them, and receipts granted by them, the business books of the specified traders, and all accounts, invoices, and receipts.

The competing companies tendered the rates-books and exceptional rates-books, but along with certain of the specified traders objected to making further production on the ground *inter alia* that such production would be prejudicial to their respective interests. The Court *held* that they were not bound to produce further under the call as made.

Terms of restricted specification under which L. O. granted diligence against havers not parties and objecting.

N. B. R. v. *Garroway*, Feb. 21, 1893, 20 R. 397, 30 S. L. R. 446.

II. THE COMPANY AS CARRIERS.

A.—CARRIAGE OF GOODS.

(Ferguson, pp. 105-125.)

Obligation to Forward.—Reasonable facilities. Goods arriving after advertised time but before actual starting of train.

Circumstances in which it was held that a railway company was not liable for non-delivery of perishable goods within a reasonable time, which had been delivered for carriage one minute after advertised time of starting of a train which was delayed for eight minutes by the delay of an earlier passenger train.

Nicholls v. *N. E. R.*, April 16, 1888, 59 L. T. N. S. 137.

Detention of Goods.—Recovery of goods in Police Court under Act of Parliament. Action for consequential damage in County Court.

A person whose goods have been detained by a railway company, and who has obtained an order in the Police Court, under the Act for regulating the Police Courts in the Metropolis (2 & 3 Vict. c. 71, sect. 40), for the delivery of the goods, is not by that order debarred from pursuing by means of an action in the County Court his further claim for damages for their detention.

M. R. v. Martin & Co., 69 L. T. N. S. 353.

Warehouse Charges.—Right to sell goods to defray charges.

A plaintiff consigned certain goods to the H. station on the defendants' line to his own order. On their arrival the defendants intimated that if they remained there they would remain at his sole risk, and in their custody as warehousemen and not as carriers, "subject to the company's ordinary wharfage and demurrage charges." The goods remained there for about two years, when the defendants sold them to defray their charges. It was in evidence that the defendants sometimes insisted on and sometimes waived payment of such charges. *Held* they had power to sell to defray their ordinary charges.

Ivens v. G. W. R., 53 J. P. 148, 5 T. L. R. 193.

B.—CARRIAGE OF LIVE STOCK.

(Ferguson, pp. 126-138.)

Custody.—Secure place.

Certain cattle escaped from a yard at a railway station in which they were enclosed for the night—their despatch having been delayed owing to the necessity of obtaining a licence from the local authority for their transmission—strayed on the line, and were killed by a passing train. In an action for damages against the railway company it was proved that the fence of the yard was defective, but that the cattle had been taken from the pens and placed there for the night by the pursuer's representative. There was some evidence that warning had been given by the defenders' servants that the yard was not intended for such a purpose. It was held that the cattle were not in charge of the railway company, and the defenders were assoilzied.

Crawford v. The Portpatrick and Girvan Joint-committee, March 8, 1889, 26 S. L. R. 440.

Escape of Dog intrusted for Carriage.—Responsibility for injuries inflicted.

A dog with a collar and chain attached was delivered to a railway company at Kelso for carriage to Perth, the guard being told that it was a quiet animal. At Edinburgh, where it was placed for an hour and a half in the parcel office during change of train, it seemed to get excited. On being led towards the Perth train it showed a disposition to bite, and broke away from the porter who was leading it. It found its way to a public garden at some distance, where it was secured by the pursuer and two other gardeners and left in charge of the pursuer, when it bit him. The jury returned a verdict for the pursuer, but the Court granted a new trial on the ground that there was no evidence of fault on the part of the railway company. *Opinion,* that the injury was too remote to infer liability even if there had been responsibility for the escape.

Gray v. N. B. R., Nov. 4, 1890, 18 R. 76, 28 S. L. R. 81.

Observations upon right to recover damages and to what extent, in case of damage to cattle, where they have been depreciated in value both by neglect of owner and also by the fault of a railway company. (*See* Cave, J., p. 501.)

How v. L. & N. W. R., L. R. 1891, 2 Q. B. 496, and L. R. 1892, 1 Q. B. 391.

Alternative Rate.—Reasonable conditions. Written contract. Authority of stationmaster. R. and C. T. Act, 1854, *sect.* 7.

Cattle were carried by a railway company under a special contract signed by the consignor, at a reduced rate, the company to be free from all liability (including liability for loss, injury, or delay), unless such injury or delay should be occasioned by the intentional and wilful neglect or misconduct of the company's servants. The stationmaster at the station of despatch stated that the train would arrive at D. at a certain hour. The train arrived late, some of the cattle had died and others were seriously injured, and the plaintiff was thereby prevented from catching a market to which they were destined. There was no proof of intentional or wilful neglect or misconduct. The contracting note contained conditions disclaiming responsibility for :—

(2) Injury by animals' restlessness or restiveness.

(5) Overcrowding when at instance of owner, a waggon being deemed overcrowded when the number of animals exceeded that allowed by the company's printed regulations.

(6) Delivery in time for particular market or non-arrival of trains, unless a written undertaking should be given by an authorised servant of the company in the case.

(7) For damage above £15 per head to cattle, unless value declared and an additional charge made.

It was *held* (by C. A.) that all the conditions were reasonable, that the ordinary rate (56s. per waggon) was reasonable, and that the reasonableness of the alternative was a question for the judge and not for the jury.

Sheridan v. *M. G. W. R. C.*, June 6, 1888, 24 L. R. Ir. 146.

Negligence.—Special contract. Reasonable conditions.

The plaintiffs sent horses by an ordinary goods train to be carried on the defenders' line. There were no horse-boxes at the station, but the porters, without objection by the plaintiffs, put them into an ordinary goods waggon. The defendants have different rates for the conveyance of horses—two rates for horse-boxes and a specially reduced rate for waggons, at which the animals are to be carried at the owner's risk, and the company to be exempt from all liability except for loss or damage caused by the wilful misconduct of their servants; and at the waggon rate, in case of loss or damage, however caused, no claim exceeding £10 shall be allowed for any one horse. At the full rate for horse-boxes the defendants undertake the ordinary duties of carriers. This condition, among others, was indorsed on the loading docket signed by the plaintiffs, and they also signed a declaration that the value of each horse did not exceed £10, and that they were delivered to the defendants for conveyance in cattle or goods waggons, and were to be carried entirely at owner's risk. The floor of the waggon was smooth, and some of the horses slipped and injured themselves during the journey.

Held that, having regard to the alternative rates, the contract of carriage was a reasonable one, and was not rendered unreasonable by the want of horse-boxes at the station, in the absence of any requisition for them by the plaintiffs.

Held also that there was not any implied condition in the contract that the waggon supplied was reasonably fit for the conveyance of horses.

Held further that the plaintiffs, having signed a declaration that the horses were under the value of £10 each, were precluded from objecting that the conditions were unreasonable, as exempting the company from liability beyond that amount, even in case of wilful misconduct.

Nevin & Farrell v. G. S. & W. R. C., 25 Nov. 1891, 30 L. R. Ir. 125.

Rates for Carriage of Cattle.—Contract. Animal accidentally killed. Sale of carcass.

The defendant sent cattle by the plaintiffs' line through from Dublin to towns in England. He deponed that he selected their line because H., a canvasser, represented orally to him that he could send twelve beasts in a waggon at small waggon rates and pay on account. The plaintiffs had three classes of waggon—small, medium, and large—with corresponding charges per waggon, varying according to size; and in contract notes signed by the defendant it was provided, *inter alia*, that the plaintiffs did not undertake to supply cattle waggons of any particular class or size, and that the charges would be for the class and size in which the cattle were actually carried. The contract notes did not specify the amount to be paid.

Owing to inconvenience or delay which would ensue in getting up small waggons, cattle forwarded by the defendant were loaded in waggons of the three classes, but in no case were more than twelve placed in a waggon, and the plaintiffs demanded the rates applicable to the waggons actually used, and 1½d. per head for disinfecting the steamer, and detained some of the cattle till paid.

Held that, even assuming there was a parole contract by H. that the plaintiffs would carry under all circumstances at the small-waggon rate, it was put an end to by the signed contract notes, and the plaintiffs were entitled to the rates demanded, and to detain the cattle in exercise of their right of lien.

A cow having been accidentally killed in sea-transit, and the carcass not claimed by the defendant's agent present on arrival of the boat, the plaintiffs sold it to the best advantage.

Held they were not liable in damages.

L. & N. W. R. v. Hughes, Nov. 7, 1889, 26 L. R. Ir. 165.

C.—Passengers' Luggage.

(Ferguson, pp. 139-147.)

Decision of Court of Appeal (referred to Ferguson, p. 143) *affirmed.* Observations on *Bergheim* v. *S. E. R.*, 3 C. P. D. 221. *G. W. R.* v. *Bunch*, L. R. 13 App. Ca. 31.

Cloakroom.—Contract of bailment. Condition on ticket. Misdelivery. Loss of property exceeding value of £5.

The owner of a bag exceeding the value of £5 deposited it for safe custody in a railway station cloakroom, paying 2d., and receiving a ticket with the following condition, of which he had notice, upon it:—"The company are not to be answerable for loss or detention of, or injury to, any article or property exceeding the value of £5, unless at the time of its delivery to them the true value and nature thereof be declared by the person delivering the same, and a sum at the rate of 1d. for every 20s. of the declared value be paid for such article of property for each day or part of a day for which the same shall be left, in addition to the above-mentioned charge." The bag was delivered by mistake by a servant of the company to a wrong person, and never recovered.

Held, in an action by the owner to recover from the company the value of the bag, that as the word "loss" in the 1st section of the Carriers Act, 1830, and the 7th section of the Railway and Canal Traffic Act of 1854, the words of which were followed by the condition to be construed, had been held to include "misdelivery," the word "loss" in the condition must be construed as having the same meaning, and judgment must be entered for defendants.

Skipwith v. *G. W. R.*, 7th June 1888, 59 L. T. N. S. 520.

Bag deposited in Cloakroom.—Absence of condition restricting liability.

A bag containing £10 in money was deposited in the cloakroom of a railway company's station. The owner paid 1d., and obtained a ticket acknowledging the receipt of the bag, but not containing any condition limiting the company's liability. He did not inform the clerk in charge that the bag contained money.

There was not, in the opinion of the Court, any negligence in the way the bag was fastened. The money was abstracted while the bag was in the cloakroom.

It was *held* that the railway company were liable for the amount.

Roche v. *Cork, Blackrock, and Passage R. C.*, March 20, 1889, 24 L. R. Ir. 250.

Receipt for Excess Luggage.—Rates for carriage. Conditions absolving from liability for delay. Invalid chair held not to be personal luggage.

Cusack v. *L. & N. W. R.* (No. 2), 7 T. L. R. 452.

D.—CARRIAGE OF PASSENGERS.

(Ferguson, pp. 148-207.)

Accident.—Reasonable facility for public purpose. Contributory negligence.

A passenger travelling by night, and feeling unwell, put her head out of the window of a railway carriage. She was struck by a mail-bag hanging on an apparatus supplied and erected at the side of the railway by the Postmaster-General, to whom the company was bound by statute to give all reasonable facilities for the delivery of the mails. The mail-bag hung at a distance of eight or ten inches from the window. Apparatus of the same kind had been in use on all the principal railway lines for more than thirty years without any accident having resulted. The passenger was rendered insensible, and died next morning. In an action of damages brought by her mother, the jury found for the defenders, and the Court refused a rule, holding that, the arrangement not being one from which danger was to be anticipated, it was one to which the railway company were bound to consent as a reasonable facility for the delivery of the mails. *Held* also (*per* Lord Shand) that the passenger was guilty of contributory negligence in putting her head so far out of the window.

Pirie v. *C. R.*, July 16, 1890, 17 R. 1157, 27 S. L. R. 973.

Accident.—Leaving train in motion. Duty of company to light station.

A train reached its destination at 12.40 A.M. on a dark night in August. It drew up to the platform so gently that the pursuer left his carriage, in the belief that it had stopped, while it was yet in motion, was knocked down by the door and severely injured.

It was averred that the portion of the platform where the carriage stopped was in total darkness; that the arrival platform, which extended for 200 yards beyond the covered station, was insufficiently lighted, there being only five lamps for the whole of this distance; and that of these only the two next the covered station were lit at the time. It was *held* (by Lords Rutherfurd-Clark and Lee, Lord Young dissenting) that the case should go before a jury, the questions to be submitted being, "first, whether the pursuer honestly believed that the train had stopped; and, second, whether that belief was induced by the failure of the defenders to provide lamps."

Roe v. *G. & S. W. R.*, 17 R. 59, 27 S. L. R. 38.

Accident.—Duty to warn. Contributory negligence.

In an action for damages against a railway company, raised by a passenger for injuries received in alighting at night from a train at a railway station, it was proved that the train was of unusual length; that the last carriage, in which the pursuer was travelling, was stopped opposite the end of the platform, which sloped down to the level of the rails; that the pursuer had failed to observe this when she stepped out of the carriage. The guard deponed that he had shouted to the passengers to keep their seats before the pursuer left the carriage, but in this he was contradicted. The jury found for the pursuer, and it was *held* by the Court (1) that in the circumstances it was the duty of the defenders to have given warning to the passengers to keep their seats; and (2) that the question whether they gave such warning or not was one for the jury.

Aitken v. *N. B. R.*, May 22, 1891, 18 R. 836, 28 S. L. R. 638.

Negligence.—Accident caused by fault of railway servant, not acting within scope of his employment.

A railway servant, after being dismissed from work for the day, travelled home, in breach of rules, in a guard's van. He left the door open, and a passenger looking out of the window of a passing train was struck by it and killed. Case withdrawn from jury by L. C. J., and *judgment* for defendants.

Bohl v. *Metr. R. C.*, Oct. 25, 1890, 7 T. L. R. 2.

Cf. as to temporary control by Post Office authorities—

Anderson v. *Glasgow Tramway Co.*, 19 Dec. 1893, 1 S. L. T. 384.

Injury to Passenger.—Nervous shock resulting from fright only.

Question as to whether, in view of case of *Coultas*, L. R. 13 App. Ca. P. C. 222, damages can be recovered for nervous shock resulting from fright alone. (See *infra*, p. 43.)

Wood v. *N. B. R.*, 28 S. L. R. 130.

Injury to Passenger. –Shock without physical impact. Fright. Remoteness of damage.

In consequence of a train which was too heavy for an incline being divided, and the portion in which she was seated being subsequently pulled up with a jerk in circumstances of an alarming character, a plaintiff proved that she was put in great fright by the occurrence (she was thrown down by the jerk), and that she suffered from nervous shock in consequence of such fright. She could not perform her ordinary avocations, and medical witnesses were of opinion that her symptoms might result in paralysis.

It was *held* that the judge rightly charged the jury that if great fright was, in their opinion, a reasonable and natural consequence of the circumstances in which the defendants had placed the plaintiff, and she was actually put in great fright by these circumstances, and if injury to her health was, in their opinion, a natural and reasonable consequence of such great fright, and was actually occasioned thereby, damages for such injury would not be too remote, and might be given.

Byrne v. *G. S. & W. R. of I.* (C. A. Ireland, 1884, unreported) followed, in preference to *Victorian R. Comrs.* v. *Coultas*, L. R. 13 App. Ca. 222.

Bell v. *G. N. R. of I.*, May 7, 1890, 26 L. R. Ir. 428.

Accident.—Negligence. Reasonable facilities for alighting from carriage not provided.

Wharton v. *L. & Y. R. C.*, 5 T. L. R. 142.

An infant born deformed on account of injuries sustained while en ventre sa mère, in a railway accident, cannot maintain an action for damages therefor against the railway company.

Walker v. *G. N. R. of I.*, Nov. 7, 1890, 28 L. R. Ir. 69.

Damages awarded for death of Stepmother.

Johnston v. *G. N. R.*, 26 L. R. Ir. 691.

Negligence.—Duty to passenger. Protection from violence by fellow-passengers.

A plaintiff had been employed in the eviction of pitmen from their houses, and had thereby incurred the illwill of the pitmen in a neighbourhood in which he had occasion to travel. When he took his ticket the defendants' servants had no notice that he was exposed to greater danger than the rest of the travelling public. Before the train started he was threatened, in the hearing of some of the defendants' servants, with violence by a number of pitmen at the station, and got into the guard's van for safety, but was removed and placed in a third-class carriage by the defendants' servants, who by this time knew that he had been engaged in the evictions and feared violence from the pitmen; pitmen crowded into the compartment where he was, thereby greatly overcrowding it; the defendants' servants, when applied to by him, did nothing towards attempting to get the pitmen out, or to get the plaintiff a seat in another carriage: he was assaulted and injured by the pitmen during the journey to the first station at which the train stopped; at that station the pitmen got out, and others got into the compartment and repeated the assaults upon him. This happened at each station where the train stopped, and at each station he complained to the guard, who did nothing to secure his safety. He sued the railway company for damages.

Held (by Q. B. D.) that there was no evidence of a breach by the defendants of any duty to the plaintiff arising out of the contract of carriage, and therefore they were not liable.

Pounder v. *N. E. R.*, Nov. 13, 1891, L. R. 1892, 1 Q. B. 385, 61 L. J. Q. B. 136.

Negligence.—Robbery of passenger. Refusal to detain train. Overcrowding of carriage.

A plaintiff averred that while a passenger in one of the defendants' trains, which was then stopping at a station, he was robbed by a gang of men who entered the carriage in which he was seated: that there was a force of police at the station at the time; that the plaintiff complained to the stationmaster of the robbery, but he refused to detain the train to permit the plaintiff to give the said men into custody and have them searched; that upon the plaintiff's complaint being made to him, the stationmaster gave the signal to start the train, which was accordingly started; that the plaintiff was thereby prevented from having the said men searched and his property recovered; and that the stolen property was in the carriage when he complained to the stationmaster, and might and would have been recovered if he had afforded time for the necessary search.

Held that the statement of claim disclosed no cause of action.

Cobb v. *G. W. R.*, Feb. 6, L. R. 1893, 1 Q. B. 459,
62 L. J. Q. B. 335.

DAMAGES AND DILIGENCE.
(Ferguson, pp. 178-182.)

Damages.—Remoteness.

A passenger claimed to recover as damages from a railway company a sum of money of which he had been robbed, in consequence, as he alleged, of the company's negligence in allowing their carriage to be overcrowded.

Held that the damage claimed for was too remote.

See *Cobb* v. *G. W. R.*, *supra*.

Damages.—Discharge.

A commercial traveller injured in a railway accident accepted a sum of £27, and granted a receipt bearing that it was "in full of all claim competent" to him. Eighteen months after he raised an action concluding for £5000. The company pleaded that in respect of the receipt they were entitled to be assoilzied.

In a proof evidence was led, bearing upon the granting of the receipt and the pursuer's state of mind and body. The L. O. awarded £500, and the Second Division adhered. The House of Lords, being of opinion that the writing was a discharge, that there had been no attempt to mislead, that the pursuer was capable of understanding it, and that there had been no understanding that there was any reservation of claims, reversed and assoilzied.

N. B. R. v. *Wood*, July 2, 1891, 18 R. (H. L.) 27,
28 S. L. R. 921 (*rev.* C. of S. p. 130).

Damages.—Excess.

The court will be slow to set aside a verdict on the ground of excess of damages where it cannot be shown that the jury took into account elements which they were not entitled to take into account.

Observations as to the elements a jury might legitimately take into account, it being judicially admitted that the pursuer had suffered no "specific loss to his business in consequence of the injury sustained."

Circumstances in which the court refused to disturb a verdict for £1800.

M'Laurin v. *N. B. R.*, Jan. 5, 1892, 19 R. 346, 29 S. L. R. 291.

Excess.—Door not properly fastened. Damages reduced of consent.
Middlemass v. *N. B. R.*, 12th May 1893, 1 S. L. T. 12.

Diligence.—Business books. Income-tax receipts.

Diligence granted to recover a pursuer's business books for three years, and his income-tax receipts for same period, he averring that his business had suffered owing to his having received personal injuries.

(*Craig* v. *N. B. R.*, 15 R. 808, distinguished.)
Johnston v. *C. R.*, Dec. 22, 1892, 20 R. 222, 30 S. L. R. 222.

Diligence.—Report by stationmaster.

Injuries received while alighting at station. Diligence to recover the report made at the time by the stationmaster to his superiors *refused*.

Macfarlane v. *G. N. S. R.*, 1 S. L. T. 127.[1]

Warrant to cite Skilled Witnesses in England.

Warrant to cite examining doctors refused, but attending nurses granted.

Macdonald v. *H. R.*, Dec. 17, 1892, 20 R. 217, 30 S. L. R. 201.

DETENTION OF TRAINS. (Ferguson, pp. 183-188.)

Detention of Trains.—Sleeping Car Co. Contract for berth. Warranty of punctuality. Representation of times of arrival of trains.

A statement in official guide, by a company having cars on certain trains, that such trains correspond with others leaving a certain place at a specified time, is not a warranty but a mere representation, and imposes no duty on the company to see that such trains do so arrive.

Lockyer v. *Int. Sleeping Car and European Express Trains Co.*, May 3, 1892, 61 L. J. Q. B. 501.

FARES AND TICKETS.—REMOVAL, ETC.
(Ferguson, pp. 188-207.)

Right to Remove.

In an action for damages for illegal expulsion from a railway carriage, it appeared that a ticket-collector had without objection received from one passenger in a carriage tickets as for all the occupants of that carriage. Having discovered a few minutes later that one of the tickets was defective, he returned and de-

[1] Similar decision by First Division on wider specification: *Silver* v. *G. N. S. R.*, 23rd January 1894.

manded payment from the passenger who had handed over the tickets. On refusal the passenger was forcibly taken out of the carriage and to the ticket-collector's office, from which he was dismissed after giving his name and address. It was held that the railway company had no right to remove the passenger from the train, their claim, if any, being one to be enforced by ordinary process of law. *Opinions* to the effect that a person so collecting tickets from fellow-passengers and handing them to the official does not incur responsibility of any kind.

Harris v. *N. B. R.*, June 30, 1891, 18 R. 1009, 28 S. L. R. 751.

Forcible Removal of Passenger from Carriage by Company's Servants.—Implied authority. Assault.

There is an implied authority by a railway company to its servants to remove passengers from carriages in which they are misconducting themselves, or travelling without having paid the proper fare. A railway company is, however, liable for the acts of its servants if in pursuance of such authority, but under a misapprehension, they eject a passenger who has neither misconducted himself nor travelled improperly.

Lowe v. *G. N. R.*, June 14, 1893, 62 L. J. Q. B. 524.

Right to Detain.—Railway Regulation Act, 1889, *sect.* 5, *sub-sect.* 2.

Company held not justified in detaining a passenger who had given her name and address on being challenged for travelling without ticket, pending inquiry whether these were correct, when they turned out on inquiry to have been correctly given.

Knights v. *L. C. & D. R. C.*, 62 L. J. Q. B. 378.

Passenger Ticket used for Station other than that for which it is available. Action to recover full fare to station at which passenger alighted.

The defendant, a passenger on the plaintiffs' railway, took a ticket to S., for which he paid 8s.; the ticket contained a condition that if used for any other station it would be forfeited and the full fare charged. He alighted at F., a station short of S., to which the fare was 9s., took a ticket at F. to his destination on a branch line, and did not give up at F. his original ticket. The plaintiffs brought an action in the County Court claiming to recover 9s., the full fare to F., or 1s. if the defendant was entitled to be credited with the 8s. paid for the original ticket, but were non-suited on the ground that they were suing for a penalty which was only recoverable before justices.

Held that they were not suing for a penalty, but to recover the fare under their contract with the defendant, and that the action was maintainable. (*L. B. & S. C. R. C.* v. *Watson*, L. R. 4 C. P. D. 118, distinguished.)

G. N. R. v. *Winder*, L. R. 1892, 2 Q. B. 595, 61 L. J. Q. B. 608.

Travelling without Payment of Fare.—Demand. Criminal proceedings. Regulation of Railways Act, 1889, 52 & 53 *Vict. c.* 57, *sect.* 5, *sub.-sect.* 3 (*a*).

The respondents were summoned before a magistrate for travelling without having previously paid their fare, and with intent to avoid payment thereof. It was proved that they had travelled in a first-class carriage with second-class tickets. Evidence having been given that the excess fare had been demanded, the magistrate at once dismissed the summons, on the ground that the respondents, having been asked to pay the excess fare, could not be proceeded against criminally.

Held that this was wrong, and case remitted for further consideration.

Noble v. *Killick*, Jan. 13, 1891, 60 L. J. M. C. 61.

As to proceedings against passenger for refusing to pay fare, *cf.* case under Tramways Act, 1870, in which it was laid down that such proceedings are criminal proceedings.

Rayson v. *South London Tramways Co.*, L. R. 1893, 2 Q. B. 304, 62 L. J. Q. B. 593.

Non-production of Ticket.—Giving wrong address. Action for false imprisonment. Regulation of Railways Act, 1889, *sect.* 5, *sub-sects.* 1 *and* 2.

Brotherton v. *Metr. & Dist. Joint-committee*, Aug. 9, 1893. 9 T. L. R. 645.

Arrest and Imprisonment for refusal to show Ticket.—Reasonable suspicion of offence against Railway Cl. Act, 1845.

Young v. *S. E. R.*, Dec. 3, 1888, 5 T. L. R. 112.

Drunken Man attempting to enter Public Vehicle.—Duty of conductor. Negligence.

Delany v. *Dublin United Tramways Co.*, 30 L. R. Ir. Ex. 725, and 740.

See also the Regulation of Railways Act, 1889, sects. 1, 2, 5, 6, and 7, App. p. 69.

c

III. THE COMPANY AND THE PUBLIC.
A.—THE COMPANY AND ADJOINING PROPRIETORS.
(Ferguson, pp. 209-225.)

ACCOMMODATION WORKS.
(Ferguson, pp. 209-210.)

Determination of Disputes as to such Works by Sheriff.—Whether appeal from Sheriff-Substitute to Sheriff-Principal competent. R. Cl. Act of 1815, sects. 61 and 150.

It is not competent to appeal from the determination pronounced by a Sheriff-Substitute under sect. 61 of the Act of 1845.

Main v. The Lanarkshire and Dumbartonshire R. C., 19th Dec. 1893, 1 S. L. T. 383.

DUTY TO FENCE.
(Ferguson, pp. 210-215.)

Liability to Fence as against adjoining Land.—Sufficiency of fence. R. Cl. Act, 1845 (E.), sects. 68-73.

In 1862 a railway company acquired lands, and fenced their line by a ditch and bank with post and rails on top, the ditch being on plaintiff's side, and the bank next to the line. In 1890 the plaintiff's cow slipped into and was found dead in the ditch. *Held* that fence was properly and sufficiently constructed, and company not liable for loss of cow.

Ryan v. G. S. & W. R., 32 L. R. Ir. 15.

BRANCH RAILWAYS.
(Ferguson, pp. 213-215.)

See *Portway v. Colne Valley and Halstead R. C.*, sup. p. 12.

LIABILITY FOR DAMAGE CAUSED BY WORKING OF RAILWAY.
(Ferguson, pp. 215-217.)

Fire caused by Sparks from Engine.—New type of engine. Spark-arrester.

The owners of a flax-store near the line of the C. R. Co. brought an action against the company for damages on account of the destruction of the store, which had been set on fire by a spark from one of the company's engines. The pursuers alleged that the engine was improperly constructed in respect that it had no "spark-arrester." The evidence showed that spark-arresters were in common use at one time, but in the case of engines of a modern type, such as the engine which had caused the fire, they had been discontinued, both because they impaired the efficiency of the engine, and because other means were adopted of preventing the emission of sparks, which the defenders' witnesses—a number of locomotive engineers—alleged were as efficacious as spark-arresters; and it was proved that the use of spark-arresters had been given up by most of the larger English railway companies. The pursuers, on the other hand, adduced witnesses who deponed that in their opinion spark-arresters ought to be used in modern engines.

Held that it was not proved that the defenders were negligent in using an engine which had no spark-arrester, and therefore they fell to be assoilzied.

Observed, per Lord President, that it is a rule fixed by a long series of decisions that a railway company is not liable in damages for a fire caused by one of its engines unless it is proved that the company was negligent.

Opinion, per Lord M'Laren, that railway companies are not under a legal disability to improve the efficiency of their engines, merely because such improvement may tend in some small degree to increase the risk of setting fire to adjacent property.

Port-Glasgow and Newark Sailcloth Co. v. C. R., March 15, 1892, 19 R. 608, 29 S. L. R. 577; aff. by H. L., 21st Jan. 1893, 20 R. (H. L.) 35, 30 S. L. R. 587.

Engine Fires.—Damage by sparks.
Groom v. G. W. R., Jan. 23, 1892, 8 T. L. R. 253.

RIGHTS AND OBLIGATIONS IN REGARD TO MINERALS IN VICINITY.
(Ferguson, pp. 218-221.)

Mines and Minerals.—Shale in banks of cutting.

Terms of Special Act and Disposition following, under which *held* that a railway company were not the owners of the "minerals," including under that term "shale," above the formation level of the railway, forming part of the sides of cuttings through which the railway ran, and within the company's fences. (*Nisbet Hamilton v. N. B. R.*, 13 R. 454, distinguished.)

Earl of Hopetoun v. N. B. R., 17th May 1893, 20 R. 704, 30 S. L. R. 622.

Mines and Minerals.—Freestone. Railway Clauses Act, 1845, sect. 70.

Held that freestone falls within the exception of "mines of coal, ironstone, slate, or other minerals" in the 70th section of the Act of 1845, and was not carried to a railway company, which had acquired lands under the powers of that Act, by a disposition that did not mention mines and minerals.

G. & S. W. R. v. Bain, Nov. 15, 1893, 31 S. L. R. 98.

Right to Work under Line.—Bonâ fides of notice. Railway Clauses Act, 1845, sect. 71.

A railway company sought to interdict the lessee of a quarry who had given them notice under sect. 71 of the Act of 1845 that he intended to work the freestone under their line. They averred that in the ordinary and proper course of management said freestone could not be worked for years, and that the respondent had given them notice under the Act merely with the view of rearing up a fictitious claim.

Held that these averments were relevant, and proof *allowed.*

G. & S. W. R. v. *Bain, supra.*

Mines and Minerals.—Include those got by open workings. Limestone.

"Mines of coal, ironstone, slate, and other minerals" excepted out of a conveyance to a railway company, and the "mines or minerals" under the railway or within a specified distance which may be worked upon notice, *held* to include not only beds and seams of minerals got by underground working, but also such as can only be worked, and according to the custom of the district would be properly worked, by open or surface operations; and *held* also that limestone is a mineral.

Midland R. C. v. *Robinson,* L. R. 15 App. Ca. 19 (affirming 37 Ch. D. 386), 59 L. J. Ch. 442.

Cf. also

Consett Waterworks Company v. *Ritson,* Jan. 21, 1889, L. R. 22 Q. B. D. 318; C. A., May 1, 1889, L. R. 22 Q. B. D. 702.
Knowles v. *L. & Y. R. C.,* June 4, 1889, L. R. 14 App. Ca. 248.
L. & N. W. R. v. *Evans,* L. R. 1892, 2 Ch. 432; in C. A., L. R. 1893, 1 Ch. 16.

Minerals.—Open workings. R. Cl. Cons. Act (England), 1845, *sects.* 77, 78, 79.

A railway, which was subject to the provisions of the Railways Clauses Consolidation Act, 1845, passed over a bed of valuable clay, the manner of working which in the district was by open quarrying. The owner, who had sold the land to the company, reserving mines, gave notice to the company of his intention to work the clay, and the company did not purchase it.

Held that the owner was entitled to work the clay from the surface, and for that purpose to enter upon the land conveyed by him to the railway company, and to remove the ballast and surface soil lying above such clay.

Ruabon Brick and Terra Cotta Co. v. G. W. R., L. R. 1893, 1 Ch. 427, 62 L. J. Ch. 483.

Minerals.—Owners working minerals under line. Line coming down in consequence. Right of mineral owners to Mandamus.

A railway company took land under an agreement which reserved to the owners the minerals and clay under the land, the clay being valuable for terra-cotta works. The time for the compulsory purchase of the minerals having passed, the company offered to purchase the clay under the line, but they could not come to terms with the owners as to price, and the owners—as they had a right to do—worked the clay under the line, with the result that the line became unsafe and came down; and as the owners refused to allow the company to prop up the line with supports, the company ceased to work the line. Upon a rule obtained by the owners to compel the company to reinstate and keep open the line—

Held (1) that Mandamus is the proper remedy in such a case; but (2) that as the words in the Act were enabling and not compulsory words, there was no absolute obligation on the company either to make or maintain the line, and they could abandon the same, and that the circumstances did not justify the issue of a Mandamus in favour of persons who had themselves pulled the line down.

Reg. v. G. W. R., ex p. The Ruabon Brick and Terra-cotta Company, June 26, 1893, 62 L. J. Q. B. 553, 69 L. T. N. S. 443 and 573.

SPECIAL OBLIGATIONS. (Ferguson, pp. 221-225.)

Statutory Obligation to stop Trains.—Temporary or permanent.

A company was bound by a clause in their Act in 1855 to "erect and maintain a temporary goods and passenger station" at a point to be agreed on, on an estate which was to be intersected by their line of railway, on the narrative that the then proprietors of the estate had laid out a portion for feuing. The clause proceeded: "At the said station all ordinary trains shall stop for the purpose of traffic;" and then came a proviso that if on the expiry of five years the traffic proved unremunerative, the company should no longer be bound to maintain the said station, and that the question of the maintenance or abandonment of the station should be determined by arbitration.

A station was erected, and no proposal to abandon it was ever made. In 1858 the same parties made an agreement which proceeded on a recital of the above clause, and provided that, in consideration of certain prestations in favour of the railway company, they should complete the station as a permanent station, and should thereafter maintain it in all time coming at their own expense. Subsequently the estate was sold. In 1892 the then proprietor brought an action against the railway company to have it declared that they were bound to stop all ordinary trains, and in particular certain specified trains, at the said station on his estate.

Held (*rev.* First Division) that all ordinary trains must stop at the station.

Gilmour v. *N. B. R.*, June 23, 1893, 20 R. (H. L.) 53, 30 S. L. R. 947, L. R. 1893, A. C. 281 ; *rev.* 20 R. 409, 30 S. L. R. 450.

"*Ordinary Trains.*"
Gilmour v. *N. B. R.* (*per* L. O.), 1 S. L. T. 404.

Construction of Ventilating Shaft on Ground Feued.—Rights of co-feuars.

A piece of ground was feued to different persons by contracts practically identical. The feuars were bound to erect houses, and prohibited from carrying on any business that might be "nauseous or hurtful" to the neighbouring feuars. The North British Company, which had acquired one of the feus, applied to the Dean of Guild for authority to erect a shaft on their feu for the ventilation of a tunnel in an underground railway. Co-feuars objected. The Dean of Guild refused the petition; but the Court recalled his deliverance, *holding* that there was no contravention of the prohibitions of the feu-contract unless the proposed erection could be regarded as the carrying on of a nauseous or hurtful business, and that it was premature to decide this, and that, as regards the building obligations, there was no such mutuality between the co-feuars as to give the objectors a *jus quæsitum* to enforce them.

N. B. R. v. *Moore*, July 1, 1891, 18 R. 1021; reported as
N. B. R. v. *Whyte*, 28 S. L. R. 782.

Specific Performance.

Obligation to build up cills of side arches of bridge over large river, attended with uncertainty as to effect, and danger of flooding neighbouring country. Specific implement *refused.*

Duke of Richmond v. *G. N. S. R.*, unreported. Lord Kinnear, Ordinary, Nov. 15, 1889. In First Division, on reclaiming note against allowance of proof, May 25, 1889.

Construction.—Want of precaution in conducting dangerous operations. Railway Cl. Cons. Act, 1845, 8 Vict. c. 20. sect. 16. Interdict.

The above Act provides that it shall be lawful for the company, for the purpose of constructing the railway, to do all acts necessary for making the railway, provided always that in the exercise of the powers granted the company shall do as little damage as can be. Consequently *held* that contractors constructing a railway for a company under statutory powers, whose blasting operations had done serious damage to adjoining property, and who had failed to show that any precautions had been taken or even considered, were not protected from interdict by said section. *Gillespie* v. *Lucas & Aird*, July 14, 1893, 20 R. 1035, 30 S. L. R. 843.

Diligence.—Company and contractor. Recovery of writings passing between at instance of third party.
M‘Laren v. *C. R.*, 1 S. L. T. 42.

Works.—Obligation to reconvey to adjoining proprietor. " Necessary and convenient for traffic." Land used for a garden. Coal-shed let to tenants.

Land was conveyed to a railway company for the construction of "a stationhouse and other works and conveniences necessary and convenient for passengers and goods traffic," with a covenant by the company that if any part should not within five years be used for the purposes of the stationhouse, works, and conveniences, and so used at the expiration of that term, the company would reconvey or purchase as therein mentioned. About fifty-two perches were used as garden ground, in part by the stationmaster and in part by some of the porters, and about four perches were occupied by a coal-shed, let by the company to a coal-dealer to store his coal, brought by the railway ready for distribution.

Held that the company were not bound to reconvey or purchase. *Harris* v. *L. & S. W. R.*, March 2, 1889, 60 L. T. N. S. 392.

Sale of Surplus Land with House thereon.—Access of light through railway arches. Implied obligation to purchaser.
See *Myers* v. *Catterson*, Dec. 16, 1889, L. R. 43 Ch. D. 470, 59 L. J. Ch. 315.

B.—THE COMPANY AND THE GENERAL PUBLIC.
(Ferguson, pp. 226-240.)

Accident.—Reasonable precaution. Child killed on private harbour line.

Seven disconnected waggons were standing beside a steamer en

a line of rails leading from a railway station to a private harbour.
A boy who had been standing on a narrow space between the rails
and the edge of the quay was crushed, while attempting to cross
the line, between two waggons which had been set in motion by
a train that was being moved backwards for the purpose of
attaching the waggons. The driver of the train, which was 128
feet from the nearest waggon, had before starting it given two
loud and prolonged whistles, and moved the train at a pace not
exceeding three miles an hour. It was accompanied by two porters
on foot, one of whom had coupled two of the waggons before the
accident happened. It was *held* that no fault had been proved on
the part of the railway company.

Smith v. *H. R.*, Nov. 1, 1888, 16 R. 57, 26 S. L. R. 33
(see Ferguson, pp. 212 and 231).

*Accident.—Servant of adjoining proprietor removing waste soil by
agreement.*

A railway company by agreement with a proprietor emptied from
their waggons opposite his property quantities of waste soil. The
company's servants cleared the signal-wires at the side, the waggons
left, the line was re-opened, and the proprietor's representatives removed the soil from the embankment at their convenience. The
line having been so opened one evening, on the following morning a
workman was killed when removing soil from between the wires
and the line, he having stepped within the wire. Juries having
on two occasions found unanimously for the pursuer, his widow,
the Court twice ordered new trials on the ground that the verdict
was contrary to evidence.

Flood v. *C. R.*, Nov. 30, 1889, 27 S. L. R. 127.

Accident.—Caused by insufficient height of underline bridge.

Bridge voluntarily constructed by railway company, and road
taken over by Police Commissioners.

Circumstances in which Police Commissioners only held
primarily liable. Observations on duty of railway company.

M'Fee v. *Police Commissioners of Broughty-Ferry and C. R. and
N. B. R. Cos.*, May 16, 1890, 17 R. 764, 29 S. L. R.
675.

Accident.—Dangerous place. Special duty towards children.

A child of five was run over by an engine engaged in shunting
operations. Averments in an amended record that (1) the shunting
lye was a dangerous place; (2) children of a tender age were in

the habit of frequenting it; (3) the defender's servants knew this, and also on the occasion in question knew that the child was upon the line; (4) it was their duty before shunting to see that the child was warned off, and (5) they had failed to do so, were *held relevant*, Lord M'Laren *diss*.

Haughton v. *N. B. R.*, 29th Nov. 1892, 20 R. 113, 30 S. L. R. 111.

Accident.—Railway near docks. Reasonable precaution. Contributory negligence.

A seaman was run over by a train when crossing some lines on a quay to reach his ship. There were a number of lines, and shunting was constantly going on. The pursuer led evidence that the defenders had omitted a precaution in use at other places of the kind in not having a boy preceding every train to give warning of its approach, and no evidence was led by the defenders that such a precaution was unsuited to the nature of the traffic carried on at the place. The evidence as to the actual occurrence was contradictory, but it appeared that the pursuer must either have stepped from behind some stationary waggons on to the line where he was run over, without first looking about him, or must have stood on the rails for more than half a minute without looking round. The jury returned a verdict for the pursuer. A new trial was granted, the Court *holding* (1) that if there had been no evidence of contributory negligence, there was a case for the jury on the fault of the defenders, but (2) that, whichever account was true, there was contributory negligence.

Barnett v. *G. & S. W. R.*, Jan. 22, 1891. 28 S. L. R. 339.

Accident.—Duty to person lawfully on premises.

Person standing on platform struck by door of guard's van.

Thatcher v. *G. W. R.*, Oct. 25, 1893, 10 T. L. R. 13.

Accident.—Heap left beside road. Evidence.

A person was driving along a highway at night, when his horse shied at a heap of refuse placed by a railway company on a triangular piece of land belonging to them at an intersection of roads which had been diverted. Evidence was tendered that other horses had shied at the heap on the same day. *Held* that if the heap was of such a nature as to be dangerous by causing horses to shy, it was a public nuisance, and the evidence was that it was likely to do so, and was therefore admissible.

Brown v. *Eastern and Midlands R. C.*, Feb. 13, 1889.
L. R. 22 Q. B. D. 391.

Accident.—Defective points. Liability of company exercising running powers.

A tramway company had running powers over another tramway line. Owing to a defect in the points at the junction, which were the property of, and had been maintained by, the other line, a car upset, injured a man and killed his wife who were standing on the highway. *Held* (*per* Lord Esher) that in running their cars on the highway the company assumed responsibility for the proper condition of all the apparatus in a question with the public.
Sadler v. S. Staffordshire and Birmingham District Street Tramways Co., May 2, 1889, L. R. 23 Q. B. D. 17.

LEVEL CROSSINGS. (Ferguson, pp. 226-237.)

Railway Cl. Cons. Act (E.), 1845, sects. 46, 47, 61, 62.—Level crossing. General highway. Power of justices to order hand-rails, fences, etc.

There is no power given, by sect. 62 of the English Act of 1845, to justices to order the erection of hand-rails and fences on a road which is a carriage-road and a general highway. Its application is restricted to the bridleways and footways and highways other than public carriage-ways, mentioned in sect. 61 of that Act.
Reg. v. Schofield, May 5, 1893, 69 L. T. N. S. 313.

Level Crossing.—Accident to foot-passenger. Negligence.

Circumstances in which it was *held* there was no liability on the part of a railway company for the death of a man killed when crossing a level crossing in broad daylight, the carriage gates being shut, and there being no attempt by company's servants to prevent him crossing, and no warning of train past due, and the train which struck him being visible for 200 yards, though, after the accident, additional precautions were taken by the company.
Curtin v. G. S. & W. R. of I., July 5, 1887, 22 L. R. Ir. 219.

Level Crossing.— Contributory negligence.

A man having been killed when passing over a level crossing, the acts of negligence alleged were: (*a*) not having whistled, (*b*) obstruction of view of train by signal-post, and (*c*) the absence of a porter at the crossing.

Held that as none of these omissions was neglect of statutory precautions, the defendants were not liable.
Newman v. L. & S. W. R., 55 J. P. 375, 7 T. L. R. 138.

Level Crossing at Station.—Duty to warn passengers of approaching train. Crowther v. L. & Y. R. C., 6 T. L. R. 18.
Damages.— Too remote. Nervous shock. Level crossing.

A man driving his sister was invited by a gatekeeper to cross a level crossing when a train was due, and barely escaped being dashed to pieces. The sister fainted, and suffered for long from severe nervous shock. A jury gave damages. *Held* by the Privy Council that the damages were too remote, and the verdict could not be sustained. (*Cf.* cases of Wood and Bell, *supra*, p. 28.)
Victorian Railway Commissioners v. Coultas, L. R. 13 App. Ca. P. C. 222.

Damages.—Deduction in respect of policy of insurance.

In a Canadian appeal under Lord Campbell's Act, where a widow plaintiff was entitled to a provision constituted by a policy of insurance on her deceased husband's life, it was held that the amount of the policy was not to be deducted from the damages previously awarded.
Grand Trunk R. C. of Canada v. Jennings, L. R. 13 App. Ca. P. C. 800.

Trespassing on Railway.—Public right-of-way before making of railway. Jurisdiction of justices.

Conviction held wrong because— (1) claim of right-of-way ousted jurisdiction of justices; (2) there was no provision in the Act of Parliament extinguishing the right-of-way, which was consequently still in existence.
Cole v. Miles, 57 L. J. M. C. 132.

MAINTENANCE AND REPAIR OF BRIDGES. (Ferguson, p. 237.)

A railway company must keep not only the bridge, but the roadway, in repair, where the road is carried over the line.
L. & Y. R. C. v. Mayor of Bury, July 25, 1889, L. R. 14, App. Ca. 417 (affirming Court below : *v.* Ferguson, p. 238), 59 L. J. Q. B. 85.

GENERAL CONDUCT OF TRAFFIC. (Ferguson, p. 239.)

Carriage.—Contamination of bags of sugar by leakage from boxes containing poison in course of carriage. Liability to persons poisoned.

A railway company received for carriage a box containing tin cases filled with a poisonous but almost colourless liquid weed-killer. The box had the words "weed-killer" stencilled on it, but the consignor did not inform the company that the box in fact contained weed-killer, or that the contents were poisonous. In transferring from one waggon to another, the railway porters noticed that the box was leaking, and noted this on the way-bill. They put it into the new truck beside some bags known to contain sugar. On arrival, one of the bags was seen to be discoloured, and there was noted in the company's private way-bill, "one bag wet with dip." They did not inform the consignee, but his assistant noticed the external discolouration, which he attributed to rain. The contents of the bags were mixed, and when that from the contaminated bag was reached in retail consumption, two of the purchasers died from arsenical poisoning and others became ill. In an action against the consignors, the railway company, and the consignees, the consignors admitted liability, and the railway company were assoilzied, the Court holding (1) that the primary responsibility lay upon the consignor, who had not given information; (2) that the company had no reason to suspect the poisonous character; (3) that mere placing of the box near the sugar, and (4) the failure to tell the consignee that the bags were wet with a liquid believed to be sheep-dip, were not such delict as to make the company liable.

Cramb v. C. R. and T. M'Ewen, Jr. and Co., July 19, 1892, 19 R. 1051, 29 S. L. R. 869.

Ferry belonging to Company.—Right to exclude public from piers.

Under a private Act of Parliament a ferry was vested in parliamentary trustees, it being declared that the piers and landing places "shall be exclusively and solely used for the purpose of the ferry and passage, and for no other purpose whatsoever, unless by the permission of the trustees in writing." A later Act empowered (by sect. 31 thereof) a railway company to acquire the ferry and piers, and "all other rights and interest of the trustees in or relating to the ferry." The company was empowered (by sect. 33) to make bye-laws for the regulation of the ferry and piers, and it was declared (by sect. 34) that it should not be lawful for any person to use the piers acquired or to be constructed, nor to land there or ship therefrom any passengers or goods, "except in such manner, and under such conditions and regulations, as shall be prescribed by the company, by the bye-laws to be made by them as hereinbefore provided, and any person so using the piers or any of them without a written authority from the company . . . or under such conditions and regulations as shall be prescribed by them, shall be liable" in a penalty.

The ferry and piers were subsequently disponed to a company with which the one which had obtained the Act had been amalgamated.

In a note of suspension and interdict at the instance of this company to restrain a steamboat proprietor from using one of the piers, it was *held* that the complainers had under the above statutes a right to exclude the public from using the piers for any but proper ferry purposes, except under written authority from them.

Opinion, per L. P., that the company might make general regulations for use by the public in general, or arrangements with particular individuals, but that in all these cases their written authority was required.

Opinion, per Lord Adam, that the reference in sect. 34 was to bye-laws provided for in the preceding sections, and that the company had no power under sect. 34 to make bye-laws or to fix any rates and duties which they were entitled to levy for any other purpose whatever than proper ferry purposes.

Opinion, per Lord M'Laren, that the reference in sect. 34 was to bye-laws provided for in the preceding sections, but that it was not of much consequence, as there was a general dispensing power by giving written authority to whomsoever they pleased to use the pier, which was only controlled by the prior right of persons to use the ferry.

N. B. R. v. *Mackintosh*, July 1, 1890, 17 R. 1065,
27 S. L. R. 825.

Powers of dealing with Obstruction and Trespass.
(Ferguson, p. 240.)

See Regulation of Railways Act, 1889, sect. 7 (power of making bye-laws for maintaining order in and regulating the use of railway stations and the approaches thereto).

The Act 24 & 25 Vict. c. 97, entitled, An Act to consolidate and amend the Statute Law of England and Ireland relating to Malicious Injuries to Property, contains two sections (35 and 36) specially dealing with placing substances on railway lines, interfering with railway machinery, and obstructing engines or carriages using any railway.

The Act *held* to apply to a private railway.
O'Gorman v. *Sweet*, 54 J. P. 663.

IV. THE COMPANY AND THEIR SERVANTS.
(Ferguson, pp. 241-245.)

Accident.—Liability for. Reasonable precautions in special circumstances for safety of surfacemen.

A surfaceman in the employment of a railway company was killed, when engaged on work at a siding, by being struck by the tender of an engine which was proceeding tender first along the siding towards an engine-shed. It was necessary to take the engine thus, and the speed was not excessive. The engine-driver's view of the place where the deceased and others were working was obstructed by the coals on the tender till it was too late to avert the accident. No other precaution to warn had been taken than a whistle from the engine, but this, owing to frequent whistling and other noises at the place, had not attracted notice. The railway company was *held* responsible in respect that they had failed to take precautions for securing that the line should be cleared before engines moving tender first were allowed to pass the place where the accident occurred.

Cairns v. *C. R.*, March 19, 1889, 16 R. 618, 26 S. L. R. 485.

Accident.—Volenti non fit injuria. Contractor's servant.

A railway company agreed with a contractor that he should shunt their trucks and supply horses and men for the purpose, they providing boys when they had boys, and when they had not, the shunting to be done without boys. On one occasion one of the men had asked the company's foreman for a boy, and, he being unable to provide one, proceeded to shunt alone, and was injured by a truck running over him, the operation being dangerous when performed by a single man.

Held by H. L. that there was no evidence of breach of duty or negligence on the part of the company.

Membery v. *G. W. R.*, May 14, 1889, L. R. 14 App. Ca. 179 (but see *Smith* v. *Baker & Sons*, L. R. 1891, App. Ca. 325).

Accident to Stationmaster, improperly on line repairing his own breach of duty.—Omission to whistle.

At a small station on a single line worked on the staff system, the stationmaster omitted to obtain the staff from the driver of a goods train, which after arrival was shunted to a siding. He left the platform and crossed the line to get the staff, and while returning, and running on the six-foot way, was struck by the engine of a passenger train due at the time. The evidence as to whether this engine whistled was contradictory.

Held by C. A. that under the circumstances the omission of the engine to keep up a continuous whistle or to whistle at all (assuming it had not done so) did not constitute actionable negligence on the part of the defendants, and that on the admitted facts the accident was entirely due to the plaintiff's own negligence.

M'Donnell v. *G. S. & W. R.*, Aug. 6, 1888, 24 L. R. Ir. 369.

Reparation.—Common employment.

In an action for damages at the instance of a carter in the employment of a contractor against a railway company, the pursuer averred that while he was engaged in taking delivery from the defenders of several bales of esparto grass he was injured by one of the bales being allowed, through the fault of the defenders' servants, to fall upon him. The defenders pleaded that the action was irrelevant, the pursuer and their servants being engaged in a common employment.

Held, following *Johnson* v. *Lindsay*, L. R. 1891, A. C. 371, that the action was relevant.

M'Callum v. *N. B. R.*, Feb. 18, 1893, 20 R. 385, 30 S. L. R. 427.

But contrast with this the case of a servant lent to perform particular services, his general master parting *pro hac vice* with control.

Donovan v. *Laing, Wharton, and Down Construction Syndicate, Lim.*, L. R. 1893, 1 Q. B. 629.

Liability for defect in plant supplied by customers, *e.g.* waggons sent by carriers to be loaded. *See*—

Robinson v. *John Watson, Lim.*, Nov. 30, 1892, 20 R. 144, 30 S. L. R. 144.

Guard of Goods Train.—Whether a "workman" in the sense of the Truck Acts.

A plaintiff was in the employment of a railway company as guard of a goods train. His main duty was to guard and conduct the train and to marshal the trucks, but it was also part of his duty at times to assist in coupling and uncoupling the trucks and in unloading them. Having left the company's service, he brought an action to recover the amount of deductions made from his wages to a sick and funeral allowance fund, alleging that they were illegal under the Truck Acts.

Held that he was not "a workman" as defined by sect. 10 of the Employers and Workmen Act, 1875, and therefore not a person to whom the provisions of the Truck Acts (1 & 2 Will. IV., c. 37, and 50 & 51 Vict. c. 46) applied.

Hunt v. *G. N. R.*, Jan. 26, 1891, L. R. 1891, 1 Q. B. 601.

Goods Guard and Porter.—Written contract for deduction from wages. Truck Act, 1831, sect. 23. Truck Amendment Act, 1887, sect. 6.

A porter on entering the service of a railway company signed an agreement, one of the conditions of which was that certain deductions should be made weekly from his pay as his contribution to a sick and funeral allowance fund: the fund was for the benefit of the defendants' servants, and was managed by the defendants on their behalf. Deductions were made weekly from the plaintiff's wages until he left their service, when he brought an action to recover the amount as being in contravention of the Truck Acts. During the period in respect of which he sued, a larger sum had been paid from the fund for medical attendance on himself and his wife than the total amount sued for.

Held that sect. 6 of the Act of 1887 did not apply to written contracts excepted by sect. 23 of the Act of 1831, and that the deductions were legally made.

Lamb v. *G. N. R.*, 7th April 1891, L. R. 1891, 2 Q. B. 281.

Libel.—Privileged occasions. Publication to company's servants of offences committed by other servants, with names of offenders and punishments inflicted.

A railway company dismissed a guard from their service, on the ground that he had been guilty of gross neglect of duty, and published his name in a printed monthly circular addressed to their servants, stating in it that he had been dismissed, and the grounds of his dismissal.

Held that the statement was made on a privileged occasion, and that the railway company incurred no liability.

Hunt v. *G. N. R.*, May 1, 1891, L. R. 1891, 2 Q. B. 189.

See the Railway Regulation Act, 1893 (Hours of Labour of Railway Servants), App. p. 75.

V. THE COMPANY AND THE CROWN.

(Ferguson, pp. 247-258.)

Post Office.—*Misappropriation by railway company's clerks of money paid for transmission of telegraph message by the senders.*
N. E. R. v. Reg., 6 T. L. R. 15 (aff. 5 T. L. R. 429).

Post Office Parcels Act, 1882.

A steam tramway *held* not to be a railway within the meaning of this Act.
Clogher Valley Tramway Co. v. The Queen, 30 L. R. Ir. 316.

See The Conveyance of Mails Act, 1891, App. p. 77.

VI. THE COMPANY AND CONTRACTORS FOR THE EXECUTION OF WORKS.

Contract.—Clause of reference. Whether claim of damages excluded.

A specification for the construction of a line of railway contained provisions for the remeasurement when finished and payment at the scheduled rates of the whole works; for the measurement and payment of any other description of works ordered, at rates to be fixed by the engineer, whose decision was to be final and binding, and for the reference of any disputes arising as to the true intent and meaning of this specification, or as to any other matter connected with the contract to follow hereon (except those specially referred to the engineer), to an arbiter named.

The contract substituted the arbiter for the engineer (the arbiter being, in fact, the engineer) as referee under the special provisions, and contained a general clause of reference referring to him "all disputes and differences in any way connected with or arising out of the execution of, or failure to execute, the works hereby contracted for." The work was to be completed at a fixed time under penalties, and the engineer to furnish the contractor with plans and drawings for the work from time to time as it proceeded.

After completion the contractor brought an action against the railway company, concluding (1) for the price of certain altered or extra work involving remeasurement of some unadjusted items, and (2) for a sum in name of damages for loss incurred by the pursuer in erecting expensive temporary works, including a bridge which had been rendered necessary by the failure of the engineer to furnish the plans for a permanent bridge within a reasonable time.

The Court *held* that the first conclusion was excluded by the arbitration clause, but that the second was not, the L. P. putting his judgment on the grounds, *first*, that there was a breach of a very clearly implied obligation upon the company and their engineer, and *secondly*, that the claim in respect thereof being from its very nature a claim of damages, and the arbiter not being expressly empowered to assess damages, the reference clause did not embrace it.

M'Alpine v. Lanarkshire and Ayrshire R. C., Nov. 26, 1889, 17 R. 113, 27 S. L. R. 81.

Contract.—Disqualification. Excess. Extension of time clause. Comprehensive reference clause.

An arbitration clause provided that the arbiter should not be disqualified by being or becoming consulting engineer to the railway company. *Held* that he was not barred from acting by the fact that he had revised the specification and schedules upon which the work was done.

An arbiter, in virtue of an extension of time clause, after completion, extended the time fixed by the contract for the completion of the works, and subjected the contractor in penalties at the contract rate for the time occupied exceeding the extended period. By their claim lodged in the reference, the railway company had restricted their claim for penalties to a round sum, which was less than the amount thus given by the arbiter. It was held that the award was reducible *quoad* the excess over the restricted claim, but that, this being separable, it was only reducible *quoad excessum*.

The general reference clause referred to an arbiter named "all disputes and differences which have arisen or shall or may arise between the parties under or in reference to this contract, or in regard to the true intent, meaning, and construction of the same, or of the said specifications, conditions, and schedules, or as to what shall be considered carrying out the work in a proper, uniform, and regular manner . . . or as to any other matter connected with, or arising out of, this contract, and generally all disputes and differences in any way connected with the construction of this contract, or arising out of the execution of or failure to execute properly the works hereby contracted for or not."

The contractor was bound to complete the line of railway on 30th September 1884, under a liquidated penalty of £20 for every day's delay; but it was stipulated in the specification that 400 yards of embankment at the end of the line should not be formed until another contractor had completed the east abutment of a bridge and the diversion of a river, or until the written instructions of the engineer were received to proceed with the embankment. The contract contained a clause empowering the arbiter to extend the time for completion of the works if satisfied that the contractor was prevented from completing at the stipulated date by failure on the part of the company to give possession of ground, or by any other cause not imputable to him.

The arbiter fixed 30th March 1885 as the date when the works ought to have been completed, and found the contractor liable in penalties from that date to 1st May 1886, when they were actually completed. In an action of reduction of the decree-arbitral brought by the contractor, it was proved that the contractor had not in fact got access to the ground on which the 400 yards of embankment was to be formed till February 1886. The arbiter stated that he was satisfied that the contractor had not been ready to use the ground until he got it, and that his delay was not due to his not having had it earlier.

The Court of Session *held* that as the whole matter, including the construction of the contract, had been referred to the arbiter, the Act of Regulations precluded their interference, even on the ground of injustice. The House of Lords *affirmed*, indicating opinions that the question as to the embankment was one on which the arbiter alone had full information, and on which the presumption was that his decision was right.

Adams v. *G. N. S. R.*, June 21, 1889, 16 R. 843, 26 S. L. R. 765. Nov. 27, 1890, 18 R. (H. L.) 1, 28 S. L. R. 579, L. R. 1891, App. Ca. 31.

VII. STATUTORY POWERS FOR THE TAKING OF LANDS.

(Ferguson, pp. 259-265.)

Compulsory Powers.—*Tenant's interest. Compensation. Notice. Lands Cl. Act, sects.* 17 *and* 115.

A railway company gave notice to an agricultural tenant that they intended to take part of his farm under the Lands Clauses

Act, and that they required him to state his claim for compensation, and that they were willing to treat with him in regard to it, and at the same time demanded that if he claimed compensation under an unexpired lease he should produce the lease or other evidence along with his claim within twenty-one days, and that, failing his doing so, he would be considered as a tenant from year to year in terms of sect. 115.

Held that the company was not entitled under sect. 115 to demand production of the lease until a claim for compensation had been made by the tenant.

Forfar and Brechin R. C. v. *Bell,* May 17, 1892, 19 R. 786, 29 S. L. R. 648.

Compulsory Powers.—Acquisition of land. Servitude.

When land is taken by a railway company under compulsory powers, it is taken absolutely free of all servitudes, unless otherwise provided in the Special Act. A railway company by their private Act obtained compulsory powers to acquire land, and were taken bound to satisfy every claim competent to the town council of a burgh for the "loss of all rights of servitude of which they shall be deprived by the construction of the company's works."

Some years after the execution of the works the burgh contended that this clause by implication saved its servitude of way over a strip of ground in front of the railway station, which had been taken by the company and converted into a garden, in respect that no works had been constructed to deprive the burgh of its right.

Held that the servitude had been extinguished.

Town Council of Oban v. *Callander and Oban R. C.,* June 21, 1892, 19 R. 912, 29 S. L. R. 818.

"Superfluous Land."—Lands Cl. Act, sect. 120.

A piece of ground acquired by a railway company under compulsory powers had not been used for more than ten years after the completion of their works, and had not been sold by them. It could not be utilised by the company unless they could take additional land from the adjoining proprietor, which was beyond their statutory powers.

Held that the ground was superfluous land within the meaning of sect. 120.

Stewart v. *H. R. Co.,* March 8, 1889, 16 R. 580, 26 S. L. R. 438.

STATUTORY POWERS FOR THE TAKING OF LANDS 53

Entry on Lands.—Lands Clauses Cons. (Scotland) Act, 1845 (8 Vict. c. 19), *sects.* 17, 83, 87, 112, 114.

Penalties for entry without consent, and prior to payment or deposit, may be recovered by tenants for a year or for a shorter term, as well as by owners or tenants on long leases. *Question* (per Lord M'Laren), whether the penalty of £25 for a second offence can competently be modified by the Sheriff.

Glasgow District Subway Co. v. *Thomas Johnstone and others,* Dec. 13, 1892, 20 R. (J. C.) 28, 30 S. L. R. 324.

Entry on Land Taken, pending Appeal as to Arbiters' Award.
Lambert v. *Dublin, Wicklow and Wexford R. C.,* Feb. 11, 1890, 25 L. R. Ir. 163.

Title to Land Compulsorily taken.—Whether statutory or feudal. Casualties. Superior and vassal. Lands Clauses Cons. (Scotland) Act, 8 *Vict. c.* 19, *sects.* 80, 107, *etc.,* 117, *and* 126.

Land acquired compulsorily, and conveyances in form of statute. *Held* that no proper feudal relation was established, and that charters of confirmation subsequently obtained were inept as titles to the lands, and not pleadable as contracts fixing the compensation to the superiors.

Magistrates of Elgin v. *H. R.,* 11 R. 950, considered.
Magistrates of Inverness v. *H. R.,* March 16, 1893, 20 R. 551, 30 S. L. R. 502.

Lands Clauses Act, 1845, *sect.* 126.—*Superior and vassal.*

Railway company liable for feu-duty where lands acquired for extraordinary purposes.

M'Corkindale v. *C. R.* (Lord Low), 1 S. L. T. 239.

Limits of Deviation.—Widening of existing line.

The general provisions of sect. 15 of the English Railways Cl. Act of 1845, as to the distance to which a company may deviate from the line delineated on the parliamentary plans, and the decisions under that section to the effect that the distance is to be measured from the *medium filum viæ* of the line as actually laid down to that of the line delineated on the plans, apply only to the construction of a new, and not to the widening of an existing line.

A railway company were authorised to widen their line, and on the deposited plans the existing line was shown with dotted lines on either side indicating the limits of deviation. They constructed a portion of the widening outside one of the dotted lines, and on land taken from the plaintiff, who brought an action for an injunction but failed to show any special damage. The land taken was comprised in the parliamentary plans and books of reference, and an original notice for a part was, after a claim from the tenants that the whole should be taken, and a refusal from the landlord to sell anything he was not compelled to sell, supplemented by a second notice to take the remainder.

Held (by Kay, J.) that the company had exceeded their powers in constructing part of the line outside the limits of deviation, but (assuming this by Kay, J. and the Court of Appeal) that as the subjects were included in the plans and were reasonably necessary for the completion of the works, the company had powers to take them. The Attorney-General's powers of interference were not invoked.

Finck v. *L. & S. W. R. Co.*, L. R. 44 Ch. D. 330, 59 L. J. Ch. 458.

On lateral and vertical deviation, *cf.* :

Herron v. *Rathmines Commissioners*, 27 L. R. Ir. 179.
(*per* Fitzgibbon, L. J.)

Deposited Plans.—" *Delineated.*" *Land not enclosed on every side by lines.*

The plaintiffs were tenants of a nursery ground, through the S.W. part of which ran the central line of an intended railway as shown on the deposited plans. Only the S.W. boundary and part of the S.E. boundary of the nursery ground were delineated on the plans, the latter being carried to a point a little to the N.E. of the N.E. limit of deviation, and the paths in the ground were carefully delineated and carried on to short unequal distances beyond the same limit. The company gave the plaintiffs notice to treat for a strip of land bounded on the N.E. by an imaginary line beyond, and distant about a chain and a half from the N.E. limit of deviation. If this line had been traced on the plan, the tracings of the outer boundary of the nursery ground, and those of nearly all the paths would have stopped short of it. The plaintiffs applied for an injunction to restrain the company from taking any ground to the N.E. of the N.E. limit of deviation, as not being delineated on the plans.

Held (by C. A. reversing Kekewich, J.), that nothing to the
N.E. of the limit of deviation could be considered to be "delineated" on the plan, and that the company could not take
compulsorily anything beyond that limit.

When a company seek to obtain power to acquire a limited
portion only of a piece of land of great extent, which is not broken
up into closes, they must frame their deposited plans in such a way
as to show how much of it they mean to acquire power to take.

Dowling v. *Pontypool, etc., R. C.*, L. R. 18 Eq. 714, discussed.

Protheroe v. *Tottenham and Forest Gate R. C.*,
L. R. 1891, 3 Ch. 278.

Construction.—*Effect of Special Act expressly authorising taking of
land for specific purpose, conflicting with rights under feu-
charter. Statute. Servitude. Interdict.*

Powers expressly given to take scheduled land for widening a
railway, *held* not restricted by a clause that "nothing contained in
this Act shall prejudice or affect the rights of servitude or other
rights of the corporation, or of the vassals of the corporation in
virtue of their title deeds."

Macgregor v. *N. B. R.*, Jan. 26, 1893, 20 R. 300, 30 S. L. R. 404.

Conveyance (not statutory) of lands acquired.

Disponer held entitled to qualify warrandice clause of conveyance of lands acquired under provisions of a Special Act, by
inserting the words, "with and under the provisions of the said
Act."

N. B. R. v. *Magistrates of Edinburgh*, May 23, 1893, 20 R. 725,
30 S. L. R. 649.

Compulsory Powers.—*Effect of acquisition of land by railway
company under a Special Act, passed subsequent to an Act
prohibiting the erection of buildings beyond a general line
without consent of municipal authority.*

A railway company was empowered by a Special Act passed
subsequent to the Metropolis Management Amendment Act,
1862 (25 and 26 Vict. c. 102) to make under a street in London
a subway "with all necessary works connected therewith," and to
take and use such of the lands delineated on the deposited plans
and described in the deposited books of reference as might be

required for the purpose. The company built in the street within the limits of deviation a station, a part of which projected beyond the general line of buildings. The station was necessary for the purposes of the railway, and apart from the provisions of the Metropolis Management Act was unobjectionable, but it could have been erected within the general line of buildings without any inconvenience except a considerable increase of expense.

Held that the station being necessary the Special Act empowered the company to make it upon any of the scheduled lands lying within the limits of deviation; that the effect was to repeal sect. 75 of the Metropolis Management Amendment Act, 1862, so far as related to the station, and that there was therefore no jurisdiction to make an order under that section for the demolition of the projecting part.

City and South London R. C. v. *London County Council*, L. R. 1891, 2 Q. B. 513, 60 L. J. Q. B. 510 and 714, 60 L. J. M. C. 99 and 149.

Compulsory Purchase.—"*Lands.*" *Lands Cl. (Eng.) Act*, 1845, *sect.* 16. *M. S. & L. R. C.* v. *Sheffield and South Yorkshire Navigation Co.*, July 9, 1890, 6 T. L. R. 414.

Superfluous Lands.—*Sale. Covenant by purchaser to resell parts when required.*

Conveyance of whole plot is not invalidated by such a stipulation as to a small part.

Ray v. *Walker*, L. R. 1892, 2 Q. B. 88, 61 L. J. Q. B. 718.

Superfluous Land.—*Absolute sale. Covenant for lien until whole of purchase-money paid. Lands Cl. (Eng.) Act*, 1845, *sect.* 127.

In re Thackwray's and Young's Contract, Oct. 30, 1888, L. R. 40 Ch. D. 34.

Agreement for Purchase of Lands, "or of such portion as the Company may require."—Time within which option to be exercised. Completion of purchase.

Wentworth v. *Hull & N. W. Junction R. C.*, Feb. 13, 1891, 64 L. T. N. S. 190.

VIII. DEFICIENCY IN PUBLIC BURDENS.

(Ferguson, pp. 264-265.)

Lands Clauses Act (English), 1845, *sect.* 133.—*Liability to make good deficiencies in assessments.*

Purchase of houses outside limits of deviation to obtain withdrawal of owners' opposition. *Held* that these were "taken for the purposes of the works," and the liability attached.

Overseers of Putney v. *L. & S. W. R.*, L. R. 1891, 1 Q. B. 182 and 440.

Rating.—*Liability under Lands Clauses Act and Special Act to make good deficiencies in assessments.* "*General purposes*" *rule.*

Burrup and others v. *L. & S. W. R.*, Oct. 28, 1891, 64 L. T. N. S. 112.

IX. STATUTORY COMPENSATION.

(Ferguson, pp. 265-269.)

Railways Clauses Act, 1845.—"*Injuriously affected.*"

A railway company authorised by a Special Act to construct railways in a large city was, by one of its clauses bearing to be for the protection of the corporation, bound to make such alterations on sewers affected by the construction of the railway as the corporation might consider necessary. Damage was caused to property by the construction under these provisions of sewers beyond the limits of deviation, and the owner claimed compensation. It was *held* that as such damage was not caused by the construction of the railway he was not entitled to compensation under section 6 of the Railways Clauses Act of 1845.

C. R. v. *M'Bride*, Dec. 8, 1891, 19 R. 255, 29 S. L. R. 208.

The subsequent construction of an opening of 1500 feet area as a ventilator for an underground station, collecting and issuing noxious gases, *held* such an alteration in the construction and execution of the company's works as to entitle a lessee of a house to compensation for additional depreciation.

Attorney General and Hare v. *Met. R. C.*, 62 L. J., Q. B. 453.

This judgment was reversed on appeal, Dec. 4, 1893, 10 T. L. R. 134.

Lands Clauses Act, 1845, *sect.* 139.—*Competency of appeal from Sheriff.* "*Fronts or abuts.*"

Glasgow Subway Co. v. *Provan*, 1 S. L. T. 60.

*Compensation. Injuriously affected. Railways Clauses (Eng.) Act,
1845, sect. 16.*

Injury by obstruction to light. Extent to which compensation claimable. Per Lord Esher, M. R., "the words 'full satisfaction for all damages' are to give not only that which would be legal damages in an action, but compensation for all the damage which the property has in fact suffered."

In re London, Tilbury, and Southend R. C. v. Trustees of Gower's Walk Schools, L. R. 24 Q. B. D. 326. 59 L. J. Q. B. 162.

"*Injuriously affecting*" lands held therewith.

Cowper Essex v. *Local Board for Acton,* Feb. 25, 1889, H. L., 58 L. J. Q. B. 594.

Compensation.—Compulsory purchase from conservators of river. Compensation assessed by arbitration. Lands Clauses Consolidation Acts. Award impeached as having assessed compensation on wrong principles. Principles on which compensation ought to be assessed in such cases.

Conservators of River Thames v. *London, Tilbury, and Southend R. C.* 68 L. T. N. S. 21.

Compensation.—Statutory right to commit damage. Failure of special statutory tribunal. Jurisdiction of ordinary Court.

Where a right is given by statute to do acts causing damage to other persons' property subject to the payment of compensation to such persons, and the statute provides a special tribunal for assessing the compensation, if such tribunal becomes non-existent, a person whose property is damaged by the exercise of the statutory right is entitled to have the amount of compensation assessed in the High Court of Justice.

Bentley v. *M. S. & L. R. C.,* L. R. 1891, 3 Ch. 222.

Compensation.—Basis of assessment in case of copyhold lands upon enfranchisement.

See—

Lowther v. *C. R.,* L. R. 1891, 3 Ch. 443, L. R. 1892, 1 Ch. 73, 61 L. J. Ch. 108.

Marquis of Salisbury v. *L. & N. W. R.,* Dec. 18, 1879, L. R. 1892, 1 Ch. 75.

Compensation.—Interest in land. Person in occupation under building agreement. Execution of building being suspended.
See—
Birmingham and District Land Co. v. *L. & N. W. R.*, Nov. 27, 1888,
L. R. 40 Ch. D. 268.

Purchase of Land under knowledge of Building Agreements providing for Leases to be eventually granted.—Implied waiver of obligation to complete. Company's liability for compensation.
L. & N. W. R. v. *Boulton*, 63 L. T. N. S. 727.

Compensation.—Land taken compulsorily or injuriously affected. Reg. of Railways Act 1868, sect. 41. Trial in Superior Court.

Judge and jury have no jurisdiction to determine the title of the compensation, but only the amount.

In re The East London R. C., Oliver's Claim, L. R. 24 Q. B. D. 507, 63 L. T. N. S. 147.

Compensation.—Mode of assessing. Court has no power to grant a new trial of an issue directed under sect. 41 of the Regulation of Railways Act, 1868.
Birmingham and District Land Co., v. *L. & N. W. R.*,
L. R. 22 Q. B. D. 435.

X. INTERFERENCE WITH ROADS AND STREETS.
(Ferguson, pp. 269-271.)
Exercise of Statutory Powers.—Claim for damage excluded.
Right to compensation.

A company in constructing a railway through a town interfered with the level of a street. Their private Act provided that they should not alter the level of any street without the consent of the board of police. In another clause they were required to give notice to the board of any works affecting any of the streets, and to restore the street to its original level, it being provided in case of any difference between the board and the company that the question should be referred to an arbiter. In the case of the street in question the arbiter had found that it had been restored. An individual proprietor, no part of whose property had been taken, brought an action for declarator that the levels of the street had been wrongfully altered, and for decree ordaining the company to restore it to its old level, and alternatively for damages. It was *held* that the pursuer had no title to sue, and that the company having acted in conformity with the statute could not be liable in damages. *Observed* that the pursuer might have a claim for compensation under the Railways Clauses Act if his property was injuriously affected.

Muir v. *C. R.*, June 21, 1890, 17 R. 1020, 27 S. L. R. 806.

Provision for reference under Private Act.

A railway company were empowered for purposes of construction temporarily to stop up certain streets and "to use and appropriate" any of the streets so stopped under certain conditions as to the extent of the spaces occupied, and the distance of enclosures from each other. There was a clause providing for reference of disputes between the company and the corporation of the city to an arbiter. In the course of their work the company claimed to be entitled to occupy portions of a street with their materials in addition to the parts occupied by their enclosures. The corporation maintained that this was outwith the Act, and also contrary to a local Police Act. It was *held* (*dub.* L. J. C.) that a difference had arisen which must be referred to the arbiter, and that an application for interdict was incompetent.

Magistrates of Glasgow v. *C. R.*, June 17, 1892, 19 R. 874, 29 S. L. R. 769.

Compulsory Powers.—Taking road. Default in making substituted road. Injunction.

Brcke v. *Stratford-on-Avon R. C.*, W. N. (1890) 126.

XI. CONSTRUCTION AND ABANDONMENT OF WORKS.

(Ferguson, pp. 272-274.)

Construction.—Power to take temporary possession of land. Necessary purpose. Road. Railroad. R. Cl. Act (England), sect. 32.

The authority given by s. 32 of the R. Cl. Cons. Act (England), 1845, to take temporary possession of lands for the purpose of forming roads does not include taking for the purpose of forming a railroad. Land can only be so taken when the taking is necessary, and mere saving of expense does not constitute necessity. (It was in this case the intention of the company to connect the line in course of construction with an existing line by a loop line, for the purpose of bringing materials from the main line to be used in construction.)

Morris v. *Tottenham and Forest Gate R. C.*, L. R. 1892, 2 Ch. 47, 61 L. J. Ch. 215.

Abandonment.

See Miscellaneous cases *infra*, pp. 67 and 68.

XII. CONSIGNED COMPENSATION AND EXPENSES.

(Ferguson, pp. 274-275.)

Expenses.—*Liability of promoters for expenses of reinvestment of consigned money. Lands Cl. Act,* 1845 (8 Vict. c. 19), *sects.* 67 *and* 79.

In application by M. C. trustees for authority to uplift and invest in any way authorised by marriage contract, or prescribed by the Trusts Acts, or in purchase of heritable subjects, *held*—

(1) That the trustees were "absolutely entitled" under sect. 67 ; but

(2) That under sect. 79, they were not entitled to receive from the promoters the expenses of reinvestment as craved.

Opinion that the promoters are not liable in expenses unless authority is expressly given to invest in one of the particular investments there specified.

Glover and others, Feb. 24, 1893, 30 S. L. R. 658.

Expenses.—*Application of purchase-money.* 8 *Vict. c.* 19, *sect.* 79. *Entail.*

In an application by an heir of entail to uplift money consigned for lands compulsorily purchased, and to apply *pro tanto* in payment of a bond and disposition in security over the entailed estate, *held* that the railway company were not liable for expenses incurred in connection with the preparation, execution, and recording of a partial discharge and deed of restriction by the creditor in the bond.

Stirling Stuart v. *C. R.*, July 8, 1893, 20 R. 932, 30 S. L. R. 812.

Lands Cl. Act, 1845.—Arbitration. Expenses. Arbiter's Fee.
Macandrew, Wright & Murray v. N. B. R., 1 S. L. T. 142.

Payment out of money paid into Court for settled land taken.
In re Smith, Ex p. L. & N. W. R. and M. R., Nov. 19, 1888,
L. R. 40 Ch. D. 386.
Cf.—
In re Brooshooft's Settlement, July 13, 1889, L. R. 42 Ch. D. 250,
58 L. J. Ch. 654.
Ex p. Perpetual Curate of Bilston, 36 W. R. 460.

Lands Cl. Act, 1845, sect. 79.—Petition for investment of sum awarded to heir of entail as compensation. Liability of R. C. for expenses of process.
Logan Petitioner, Feb. 15, 1889, 26 S. L. R. 521.

Compulsory Purchase.—Reinvestment of purchase-money. Costs. Lands Clauses Act (England), sect. 80.
Attorney-General v. St. John's Hospital, Bath,
L. R. 1893, 3 Ch. 151.

Compulsory Purchase.—Railways (Ireland) Act, 1860. Purchase-money lodged in Court. Interest. Annuitant. Consent. Costs.
In re Dublin, Wicklow, and Wexford R. C. ex p. Jordan, 27 L. R. Ir. 79.

XIII. THE COMPANY AND ITS CREDITORS.

(Ferguson, pp. 275-277.)

Railway Companies Act, 1867.—Extension constituted separate undertaking.

When a receiver and manager has been appointed under the Act of 1867 the moneys received by him must be applied first in providing for the 'working expenses' of the railway, even though by a Special Act a fixed dividend on shares and the interest on debentures forming the capital raised for a particular undertaking are charged on the gross receipts arising from the traffic of the separate undertaking and traffic passing over both the separate undertaking and other railways of the company.

Held that a loop line having been constituted a "separate undertaking" and the capital raised for it "separate capital," yet the dividend upon and the interest of the separate capital were not "working expenses" or "proper outgoings," and must be postponed to working expenses.

Held that "working expenses" included payments for rolling stock purchased on the terms of payment by instalments at fixed periods, the stock not becoming the property of the company until the complete payment of all the instalments, and the vendor having the right to seize the stock on default in payment of any one instalment.

In re Eastern and Midlands R. C., L. R. 45 Ch. D. 367, 65 L. T. N. S. 668.

Act of 1867.—Schemes of arrangement with creditors.

In re The Brighton and Dyke R. C., L. R. 44 Ch. D. 28, 59 L. J. Ch. 409.

„ *The East and West India Dock Co.,* L. R. 44 Ch. D. 38, 58 L. J. Ch. 522.

„ *The West Lancashire R. C.,* W. N. 1890, 165, 63 L. T. N. S. 56.

Scheme of Arrangement.—Confirmation by Court. Non-assent of class of Preference Shareholders. Rights "prejudicially affected." Railway Companies Act, 1867, *sects.* 6, 10, 12, 15-17.

Held (by C. A. aff.) that the assent of the statutory majority of class to a scheme of arrangement under the Act of 1867 cannot be dispensed with under sect. 15, if any existing right of that class is prejudicially affected, it being for them and not for the Court to consider whether the scheme gives them such benefits that their rights, on the whole, are not prejudicially affected.

In re Neath and Brecon R. C., L. R. 1892, 1 Ch. 349, 61 L. J. Ch. 172.

Scheme of Arrangement.—Sale of undertaking. Bill in Parliament. Petition to sanction. Railway Companies Act, 1867.

A petition was presented for confirmation of a scheme of arrangement. Another company had agreed to purchase the undertaking, and a bill was prepared to be presented in the session of 1893 to carry out the sale. Held that the Court ought not, on behalf of unsecured creditors, to approve a scheme on the hypothesis that a Bill before Parliament would pass into law, and that petition must stand over, with liberty to apply.

In re Eastern and Midlands Co., 67 L. T. N. S. 711.

Railway Companies Act, 1867, *sect.* 23.—*Debenture-holders.
Surplus land.*

Sect. 23 of the Railway Companies Act, 1867, does not give to creditors of a railway company in respect of mortages, bonds, or debenture stock, any lien or charge which they did not possess before the Act, so as to entitle them to payment in priority out of the proceeds of surplus lands of the company which have been sold on the application of the judgment creditors of the company.

In re Hull, Barnsley and West Riding Junction R. C., Nov. 13, 1888, L. R. 40 Ch. D. 119, 58 L. J. Ch. 75.

Debenture-holders.—First charge. Gross traffic receipts. "Working expenses."

Proffitt v. The Wye R. C., May 4, 1891, 64 L. T. N. S. 669.

XIV. JURISDICTION AND ARBITRATION.

(Ferguson, pp. 277-278.)

Procedure.—Service. Scotch Railway Co. having part of its line in England. Railway Cl. (England) Act, 1845, *sect.* 138. *Companies Cl. Cons. (England) Act, sect.* 135.

A Scotch railway company, the head office of which was in Scotland, had a short part of its line in England. The Railways Clauses Act was incorporated with the Special Act of the company so far as related to the English part of the line.

Held, reversing Q. B. D., that service of a writ made at the most important office of the company on the English part of its line must be set aside, since—

(1) The defendants were *primâ facie* a Scotch company, and the incorporation of the English Act was for a limited purpose, and the fact that a part of the line was in England did not make them an English company.

(2) The defendants' principal office was that at which the control and management of the undertaking was carried on, and the service at Carlisle was consequently not service at the principal office within sect. 135 of the Companies Cl. Cons. Act, 1845.

(3) The application of order ix. 2, 8, was excluded by the incorporation in the Special Act of the statutory

provisions relating to service of process contained in the Companies Cl. Cons. (Scotland) Act, 1845.

Wilson v. C. R. (5 Ex. 822) dissented from.

Palmer v. C. R., L. R. 1892, 1 Q. B. 823, *rev.* 607.

Arbitration.

How far Court excluded by agreement to go to arbitration under Act of 1859.—*When party barred from insisting on arbitration.*

Held that Court not deprived of jurisdiction if neither party insists on arbitration.

L. C. & D. R. C. v. S. E. R. C., Nov. 6, 1888,
L. R. 40 Ch. D. 100, 58 L. J. Ch. 75.

XV. VALUATION AND TAXATION.

(Ferguson, pp. 278-283.)

Valuation Acts.—Lands acquired for railway. Embankment. Whether valued by burgh or railway assessor. Unfinished railway.

A plot of ground within a burgh had been acquired by a railway company whose Act provided that the lands from time to time acquired should "for all purposes of tolls, rates, and charges, and for all purposes whatsoever, be the undertaking railway works, and property of the company." Part of the ground had been used in the construction of a railway embankment, the remainder being covered with the debris caused by its formation. The burgh assessor had included the subjects in his valuation on the ground that they were not "wholly occupied by the railway and works," and that the railway was still unfinished. The Valuation Committee sustained, but on appeal the Court *held* that as the ground in question formed part of the undertaking of a railway company within the meaning of sections 20 and 21 of the Lands Valuation Act, 1854, the burgh assessor had no duty in regard to it and the determination was wrong.

Forth Bridge R. C. v. Assessor for Queensferry, (rep.) June 14, 1889,
16 R. 797, Jan. 31, 1889, 26 S. L. R. 533.

Income Tax.—Expenditure on permanent improvements. Deduction from revenue.

A railway company in making their return for assessment of income-tax claimed as deductions from the revenue of the year of assessment, (1) a sum expended upon the improvement of the permanent way of a line of railway which they had acquired and amalgamated with their concern in order to bring it up to the standard of the rest of the line ; (2) a sum representing the cost of the extra weight in relaying part of the main line with steel in place of iron rails and with chairs of additional weight. In the books of the company these sums were charged against capital. The Commissioners of Income-Tax disallowed the sums as deductions from revenue, holding that they were properly chargeable to capital. On appeal the Court affirmed their determination.

H. R. v. Special Comrs. of Income-Tax, July 10, 1889, 16 R. 950, 26 S. L. R. 657.

Income-Tax.—Railway company yielding no profit but paying interest on capital. Income-Tax Acts 1842 & 1853, Customs and Inland Revenue Act, 1888.
Judgment by *Lord Wellwood, Ordinary*, 17th Oct. 1890.
Lord Advocate v. *Forth Bridge R. C.*, 28 S. L. R. 576.

Railway Tunnel.— *Land tax. Liability to assessment. "Hereditament."* 38 Geo. III. c. 5, sect. 4.

The Special Act of an underground railway company provided that with respect to any of the lands taken which were in or under the roadway or footway of any street, the company should not be required wholly to take these lands or any part of the surface thereof, but they might appropriate and use the subsoil and undersurface of any such roadway or footway.

The company constructed a tunnel under the roadway and footway of a public street. In doing so, they removed the subsoil and built an arch in brickwork, with walls four or five feet thick, the foundation being permanently built in the soil. The rails of the railway were laid at the bottom of the arch. After the tunnel was constructed, the company had the sole use and occupation of it for the purposes of their railway.

Held that the right or interest of the company in the tunnel was a "hereditament."

Held (*per* Lord Esher, M. R., & Kay, L.J. (Lopes, L.J., diss.)) that the company were chargeable with land tax in respect of the tunnel.

Metropolitan R. C. v. *Fowler*, Nov. 12, 1891, L. R. 1892, 1 Q. B. 165. Decision aff. by H. L., L. R. 1893, A. C. 416, 62 L. J. Q. B. 553.

MISCELLANEOUS CASES 67

Income-Tax.—Annuity from Government. Application of balance to repayment. Revenue.
H.R.H. the Nizam State R. C. v. Wyatt, Jan 20, 1890,
L. R. 24 Q. B. D. 548, 59 L. J. Q. B. 430.

Sanitary Rate.—Partial exemption of railway company.
Kennedy v. G. S. & W. R., 30 L. R. Ir. 685 and 690.

Poor Rate.—Deficiency. "General Purposes Rate."
Burrup v. L. & S. W. R., 64 L. T. N. S. 112.

Rating.—Liability of railway company in respect of ancient river formed into a canal.
M. S. & L. R. C. v. Assessment Committee of Doncaster Union.
69 L. T. N. S. 350.

XVI. MISCELLANEOUS CASES.

Parliamentary Deposit.—Motion by lender. Promotion expenses.
Sect. 65, Co. Cl. Cons. (Eng.) Act, 1845.
Cutbill v. Shropshire Railways Co. W. N. (1891) 65,
7 T. L. R. 381.

Parliamentary Deposit.—Repayment. Abandonment.

Under Sect. 1 of the Parliamentary Deposits and Bonds Act, 1892, the Court has no jurisdiction to make an order for the repayment of a Parliamentary deposit until the time limited for the completion of the company's undertaking has expired, even though the company's compulsory powers for the purchase of land have expired, and they have raised no capital, and have taken no steps to acquire land, and have passed a resolution to abandon the undertaking.
Ex parte Chambers, Nov. 10, 1892, L. R. 1893, 1 Ch. 47,
62 L. J. Ch. 78.
Cf.—
In re Uxbridge and Rickmansworth R. C., Jan. 18, 1890, L. R. 43 Ch. D. 536, 59 L. J. Ch. 409.
In re Colchester Tramways Co., L. R. 1893, 1 Ch. 309.
In re Manchester, Middleton, and District Tr. Co., L. R. 1893, 2 Ch. 638.
Ex. p. Bradford and District Tr. Co., L. R. 1893, 3 Ch. 463, 62 L. J. Ch. 668.

Abandonment of Railway. Parliamentary Deposit. Rights of creditors and promoters.
In re Enniskillen & Bundoran R. C., Nov. 19, 1890, 25 L. R. Ir. 472.

Govt. Guarantee of 7 per cent. on Capital.—Interest at 7 per cent. on preference shares payable out of guaranteed moneys and earnings. Govt. guarantee held applicable to working expenses and maintenance of railway, and not appropriated to pay preference dividends.
Clifford v. *Imperial Brazilian R. C.*, 60 L. T. N. S. 60.

Capital contributed equally by two companies.—Mode of contribution by each company towards payment of 4 per cent. dividend thereon.
Metropolitan Railway Acts, 1879 and 1880.
Metr. Dist. R. C. v. *Metr. R. C.*, 5 T. L. R. 394 (H. L.).

Debentures.—Fund raised by. Application of Interest on.
Pope v. *M. & S. W. J. R. C.*, 6 T. L. R. 404.

Debentures.—Issue at a discount. Is legal.
Webb v. *Shropshire R. C.*, L. R. 1893, 3 Ch. 307, 69 L. T. N. S. 533.

Payment of Dividend to Shareholders out of Capital.—Rolling stock. Wear and tear of. Discretion of directors to replace.
Kehoe v. *Waterford & Limerick R. C.*, April 18, 1888, 21 L. R. Ir. 221.

Companies Clauses (Eng.) Act, 1845, sect. 18.—Transmission of shares in consequence of death.
Barton v. *L. & N. W. R*, Nov. 26, 1889, L. R. 24 Q. B. D. 77, 59 L. J. Q. B. 33.

Railway Stock.—Certificate, possession of. Certification of transfer. Equitable ownership. Priority.
Kelly v. *Munster & Leinster Bank*, 29 L. R. Ir. 19 and 41.

APPENDIX.

Railway Statutes subsequent to 1888.

Act of Sederunt for regulating Appeals from the Railway and Canal Commission.

Railway and Canal Commission Rules.

List of Cases.

Index to Supplement.

I.

REGULATION OF RAILWAYS ACT, 1889.
52 & 53 VICT. CH. 57.

ARRANGEMENT OF SECTIONS.

Section.
1. Power to order certain provisions to be made for public safety.
2. Enforcement of orders of Board of Trade.
3. Issuing debenture stock to meet expenses incurred under this Act.
4. Returns of overtime to Board of Trade.
5. Penalty for avoiding payment of fare.
6. Passenger ticket to have fare printed thereon.
7. Power to make byelaws as to stations.
8. Short title.

An Act to amend the Regulation of Railways Acts; and for other purposes.—[30th August 1889.]

BE it enacted by the Queen's most Excellent Majesty, by and with the advice and consent of the Lords Spiritual and Temporal, and Commons, in this present Parliament assembled, and by the authority of the same, as follows:

1.—(1.) The Board of Trade may from time to time order a railway company to do, within a time limited by the order, and subject to any exceptions or modifications allowed by the order, any of the following things: *(Power to order certain provisions to be made for public safety.)*

    (*a*) To adopt the block system on all or any of their railways open for the public conveyance of passengers;

(*b*) To provide for the interlocking of points and signals on or in connection with all or any of such railways;

(*c*) To provide for and use on all their trains carrying passengers continuous brakes complying with the following requirements, namely:

   (i.) The brake must be instantaneous in action, and capable of being applied by the engine-driver and guards;

   (ii.) The brake must be self-applying in the event of any failure in the continuity of its action;

   (iii.) The brake must be capable of being applied to every vehicle of the train, whether carrying passengers or not;

   (iv.) The brake must be in regular use in daily working;

   (v.) The materials of the brake must be of a durable character, and easily maintained and kept in order.

In making any order under this section the Board of Trade shall have regard to the nature and extent of the traffic on the railway, and shall, before making any such order, hear any company or person whom the Board of Trade may consider entitled to be heard.

Enforcement of orders of Board of Trade.

II. If default is made in compliance with any order made by the Board of Trade in pursuance of the last foregoing section, the Railway and Canal Commission may, on the application of the Board of Trade, enjoin obedience to the order, and thereupon the order may be enforced as if it were made by the Commission for the purpose of carrying into effect any of the provisions of the Acts under which the Commission have jurisdiction.

Issuing debenture stock to meet expenses incurred under this Act.

III. Whenever any railway company shall be ordered by the Board of Trade to provide any appliances, or execute any works, or incur any expenditure under the provisions of this Act which would properly be chargeable to capital account, it shall be lawful for such company to furnish to the Board of Trade an estimate of the cost of providing such appliances, executing such works, and carrying out such order generally, and thereupon the Board of Trade shall, upon the application of the company, fix and determine the amount which would properly be capital expenditure, and the company may from time to time issue debentures or debenture stock in priority to or ranking *pari passu* with any existing debentures or debenture stock of such company bearing interest at a rate not exceeding five per cent. per annum to an amount not exceeding the sum so fixed and determined, and any money raised under the provisions of this section shall be applied in carrying out such requirements of the Board of Trade and to no other purpose whatsoever, and no other authority save the certificate of the Board of Trade shall be requisite to authorise and validate the issue of such debentures or debenture stock.

IV.—(1.) Every railway company shall make to the Board of Trade periodical returns as to the persons in the employment of the company whose duty involves the safety of trains or passengers, and who are employed for more than such number of hours at a time as may be from time to time named by the Board of Trade. *Returns of overtime to Board of Trade.*

(2.) The returns shall be delivered at such intervals, and shall be in such form, and contain such particulars, as the Board of Trade from time to time direct.

(3) The provisions of sections nine and ten of the Regulation of Railways Act, 1871, with respect to penalties, shall apply to returns under this section. *34 & 35 Vict. c. 78.*

V.—(1.) Every passenger by a railway shall, on request by an officer or servant of a railway company, either produce, and if so requested deliver up, a ticket showing that his fare is paid, or pay his fare from the place whence he started, or give the officer or servant his name and address; and in case of default shall be liable on summary conviction to a fine not exceeding forty shillings. *Penalty for avoiding payment of fare.*

(2.) If a passenger having failed either to produce, or if requested to deliver up, a ticket showing that his fare is paid, or to pay his fare, refuses, on request by an officer or servant of a railway company, to give his name and address, any officer of the company or any constable may detain him until he can be conveniently brought before some justice or otherwise discharged by due course of law.

(3.) If any person -
(*a.*) Travels or attempts to travel on a railway without having previously paid his fare, and with intent to avoid payment thereof; or
(*b.*) Having paid his fare for a certain distance, knowingly and wilfully proceeds by train beyond that distance without previously paying the additional fare for the additional distance, and with intent to avoid payment thereof; or
(*c.*) Having failed to pay his fare, gives in reply to a request by an officer of a railway company a false name or address,

he shall be liable on summary conviction to a fine not exceeding forty shillings, or, in the case of a second or subsequent offence, either to a fine not exceeding twenty pounds, or in the discretion of the court to imprisonment for a term not exceeding one month.

(4.) The liability of an offender to punishment under this section shall not prejudice the recovery of any fare payable by him.

Passenger ticket to have fare printed thereon.

VI. From and after a date to be fixed by order of the Board of Trade, and subject to such exceptions, if any, as may be allowed by such order, every passenger ticket issued by any railway company in the United Kingdom shall bear upon its face, printed or written in legible characters, the fare chargeable for the journey for which such ticket is issued, and any railway company issuing any passenger ticket in contravention of the provisions of this section shall be liable to a penalty not exceeding forty shillings for every ticket so issued, to be recovered on summary conviction.

Power to make bye-laws as to stations.

VII. The power conferred on a railway company by the Railways Clauses Consolidation Act, 1845, and the Railways Clauses Consolidation Act (Scotland), 1845, to make byelaws subject to disallowance by the Board of Trade, shall include power to make byelaws for maintaining order in, and regulating the use of, railway stations and the approaches thereto.

Short title.

VIII. (1.) This Act may be cited as the Regulation of Railways Act, 1889.

(2.) This Act and the Regulation of Railways Acts, 1840 to 1871, may be cited collectively as the Regulation of Railways Acts, 1840 to 1889.

THE LIGHT RAILWAYS IRELAND ACT, 1889.
52 & 53 VICT. c. 66.
(*This Act does not extend to Scotland.*)

RAILWAYS IRELAND ACT, 1890.
53 & 54 VICT. c. 52.
(*This Act does not extend to Scotland.*)

Railway and Canal Traffic (Provisional Orders) Amendment Act, 1891.

54 Vict. c. 12.

An Act to remove doubts as to the Powers of Public Bodies in reference to Provisional Order Bills under the Railway and Canal Traffic Act, 1888. [11th May 1891.]

Whereas by an Act of the thirty-fifth and thirty-sixth years of the reign of Her present Majesty, chapter ninety-one, intituled "An Act to authorise the application of funds of municipal corporations and other governing bodies in certain cases," hereinafter referred to as the Borough Funds Act, authority is given to the council of any municipal borough, the board of health, local board, commissioners, trustees, or other body acting under any general or local Act of Parliament for the management, improvement, cleansing, paving, and lighting, and otherwise governing places or districts, to apply the borough fund or rate, or other the public funds or rates under the control of any such governing body, to the payment of the costs, charges, and expenses of promoting or opposing any local and personal Bill or Bills in Parliament:

And whereas by the Local Government Act, 1888, and the Local Government (Scotland) Act, 1889, the county council of an administrative county has the same powers of opposing Bills in Parliament as are conferred on the council of a municipal borough, by the above-recited Act of the thirty-fifth and thirty-sixth years of Victoria, chapter ninety-one :

And whereas by the Borough Funds (Ireland) Act, 1888, similar powers were conferred upon governing bodies in Ireland :

And whereas by the Railway and Canal Traffic Act, 1888, it was, among other things, provided that if while any Bill to confirm a Provisional Order by the Board of Trade, under section twenty-four of that Act, be pending in either House of Parliament a petition be presented against the Bill, or any classification and schedule comprised therein, the Bill, so far as it relates to the matter petitioned against, should be referred to a select committee, or, if the two Houses of Parliament think fit so to order, to a joint committee of such Houses, and the petitioner should be allowed to appear and oppose as in the case of a private Bill; and further, it was by the said Act provided that the Act of Parliament confirming any Provisional Order made under that section should be a public general Act :

And whereas doubts have been entertained, whether in view of the said enactment governing bodies, as defined by the Borough Funds Act and the Borough Funds (Ireland) Act, 1888, respectively, and county councils have power to apply the funds or rates under their control, in opposing or subscribing towards the opposition of any Bill, to confirm any Provisional Order made under section twenty-four of the Railway and Canal Traffic Act, 1888, and it is expedient that such doubts should be removed:

Be it therefore enacted by the Queen's most Excellent Majesty, by and with the advice and consent of the Lords Spiritual and Temporal, and Commons, in this present Parliament assembled, and by the authority of the same, as follows:

Powers of governing bodies and county councils with reference to Bills for confirming Provisional Orders made under 51 & 52 Vict. c. 25. s. 24.

I. Every governing body within the meaning of the Borough Funds Act or the Borough Funds (Ireland) Act, 1888, and every county council shall be entitled to be a petitioner, and to appear and oppose any Bill to confirm any Provisional Order made under section twenty-four of the Railway and Canal Traffic Act, 1888, and to provide, or contribute towards providing, the expenses of the appearance or opposition of a petitioner out of the funds or rates under their respective control, as if the Bill for confirming such Provisional Order were a local or personal Bill within the meaning of section two of the Borough Funds Act, or of section three of the Borough Funds (Ireland) Act, 1888; and the provisions of the said last-mentioned Acts, respectively, shall apply to any such appearance or opposition, and to any expenses incurred or to be incurred in relation thereto: Provided that in the case of a county council no consent of owners and ratepayers shall be required.

Short title.

II. This Act may be cited as the Railway and Canal Traffic (Provisional Orders) Amendment Act, 1891.

TRANSFER OF RAILWAYS IRELAND ACT, 1891.

54 & 55 VICT. C. 2.

(*This Act does not extend to Scotland.*)

RAILWAY AND CANAL TRAFFIC ACT, 1892.

55 & 56 VICT. C. 44.

An Act to amend the Railway and Canal Traffic Act, 1888.

[27th June 1892.]

51 & 52 Vict. c. 25.

WHEREAS by section twenty-four of the Railway and Canal Traffic Act, 1888: it is provided that after the commencement of the session of Parliament next after that in which the report of the Board of Trade, with respect to a classification of traffic and schedule of rates and charges has been submitted to Parliament, the Board of Trade may embody in a Provisional Order such classification and schedule as in the opinion of the Board of Trade ought to be adopted, and procure a Bill to be introduced to confirm the Order, and it is expedient to amend this provision:

Be it therefore enacted by the Queen's most Excellent Majesty, by and with the advice and consent of the Lords Spiritual and Temporal, and Commons, in this present Parliament assembled, and by the authority of the same, as follows:

I. A Provisional Order in pursuance of sub-section seven of section twenty-four of the Railway and Canal Traffic Act, 1888, may be made, and a Bill to confirm the same may be introduced, at any time after hearing the parties as provided in sub-section four of the said section. Time for application for Provisional Order.

II. This Act may be cited as the Railway and Canal Traffic Act, 1892. Short title.

RAILWAY REGULATION ACT, 1893.

56 & 57 VICT. C. 29.

An Act to amend the Law with respect to the Hours of Labour of Railway Servants. [27th July 1893.]

BE it enacted by the Queen's most Excellent Majesty, by and with the advice and consent of the Lord's Spiritual and Temporal, and Commons, in this present Parliament assembled, and by the authority of the same, as follows:

I.—(1.) If it is represented to the Board of Trade, by or on behalf of the servants, or any class of the servants of a railway company, that the hours of labour of those servants, or of that class, or, in any special case, of any particular servants engaged in working the traffic, on any part of the lines of the company, are excessive, or do not provide sufficient intervals of uninterrupted rest between the periods of duty, or sufficient relief in respect of Sunday duty, the Board of Trade shall inquire into the representation. Schedule of hours of labour of railway servants.

(2.) If it appears to the Board of Trade, either on such representation or otherwise, that there is, in the case of any railway company, reasonable ground of complaint with respect to any of the matters aforesaid, the Board of Trade shall order the company to submit to them within a period specified by the Board, such a schedule of time for the duty of the servants, or of any class of the servants, of the company, as will in the opinion of the Board bring the actual hours of work within reasonable limits, regard being had to all the circumstances of the traffic and to the nature of the work.

(3.) If a railway company fail to comply with any such order, or to enforce the provisions of any schedule submitted to the Board, in pursuance of any such order and approved by the Board, the Board may refer the matter to the Railway and Canal Commission, and thereupon the Railway and Canal Commission shall have jurisdiction in the matter, and the Board may appear in support of the reference, and the Commissioners may make an order requiring the railway company to submit to the Commission, within a period specified by the Commission, such a schedule as will, in the opinion of the Commission, bring the actual hours of work within reasonable limits.

(4.) If a railway company fail to comply with any order made by the Railway and Canal Commission in pursuance of this section, or to enforce the provisions of any schedule submitted to the Railway and Canal Commission in pursuance of any such order, and approved by that Commission, the company shall be liable to a fine not exceeding one hundred pounds for every day during which the default continues.

51 & 52 Vict. c. 25.

(5.) The Railway and Canal Traffic Act, 1888, shall apply in the case of any jurisdiction exercised, or order made by the Railway and Canal Commission under this Act, as if it were exercised or made under, or for the purposes of that Act: Provided that notwithstanding anything in section five of that Act, the jurisdiction of the Commission for the purposes of this Act may be exercised by the two appointed Commissioners.

(6.) The Board of Trade and the Railway and Canal Commission respectively, may from time to time rescind or vary any order made by them under this section, and make such supplemental orders as the circumstances of the case may appear to require.

(7.) This Act shall not apply to any servant of a railway company who is, in the opinion of the Board of Trade, wholly employed either in clerical work or in the company's workshops.

Annual report to Parliament.

II. A report of all proceedings under this Act shall be made annually to Parliament by the Board of Trade.

Short title.

III. This Act may be cited as the Railway Regulation Act, 1893, and shall be read with the Railway Regulation Acts, 1840 to 1889.

APPENDIX

CONVEYANCE OF MAILS ACT, 1893.
56 & 57 VICT., CH. 38.

ARRANGEMENT OF SECTIONS.

Section.
1. Differences as to remuneration for conveyance of mails.
2. Carriage of mails on tramways.
3. Carriage of mails on tramroads.
4. Determination of differences.
5. Definitions.
6. Short title.

An Act to make further provision for the Conveyance of Her Majesty's Mails. [24th August 1893.]

BE it enacted by the Queen's most Excellent Majesty, by and with the advice and consent of the Lords Spiritual and Temporal, and Commons, in this present Parliament assembled, and by the authority of the same, as follows:

I. Where under any Act relating to the conveyance of mails or under the Post Office (Parcels) Act, 1882, it is provided that any matter of difference relating to any remuneration or compensation to be paid by the Postmaster-General to any railway company shall be referred to arbitration, that matter of difference shall at the instance of any party thereto be referred to the Railway and Canal Commission instead of to arbitration, and that Commission shall determine the same, and this provision shall apply to any matter of difference referred to in section eight of the Post Office (Parcels) Act, 1882, where such railway companies as therein mentioned, or any company or person owning a steam vessel, are or is one party to the arbitration in like manner as it applies to a difference where a single railway company is a party to the arbitration. <small>Differences as to remuneration for conveyance of mails. 45 & 46 Vict. c. 74.</small>

II. (1.) Every tramway company, that is to say, every company, body, or person owning or working any tramway authorised by any Act passed after the first day of January one thousand eight hundred and ninety-three, shall, if required by the Postmaster-General, perform with respect to any tramway owned or worked by the company all such reasonable services in regard to the conveyance of mails as the Postmaster-General from time to time requires: Provided as follows:— <small>Carriage of mails on tramways.</small>

    (*a.*) Nothing in this section shall authorise the Postmaster-General to require mails in excess of the following weights to be carried in or upon any carriage, that is to say:—

        (i.) If the carriage is conveying or intended to convey passengers, and not goods or parcels, then in excess of the maximum weight for the time being fixed for the luggage of ordinary passengers; and

(ii.) If the carriage is conveying or intended to convey parcels only, then in excess of such maximum weight as is for the time being fixed for ordinary parcels, or if that maximum appears to the Postmaster-General to be so low as to exclude him from availing himself of the use of any such carriage, then as it is for the time being fixed by agreement, or in default of agreement by the Railway and Canal Commission.

(iii.) If the carriage is conveying or intended to convey both parcels and passengers but not goods, then in excess of the maximum weight for the time being fixed for ordinary parcels, or for the luggage of ordinary passengers, whichever is the greater.

(*b*.) Mails when carried in or upon a carriage conveying passengers shall be so carried as not to inconvenience the passengers, but so nevertheless that the custody of the mails by any officer of the Post Office in charge thereof shall not be interfered with.

(*c*.) Nothing in this section shall authorise the Postmaster-General to require any mails to be carried in or upon a carriage conveying or intended to convey passengers but not goods or parcels, except in charge of an officer of the Post Office travelling as a passenger.

(*d*.) If goods as well as passengers and parcels are carried on the tramway the enactments relating to the conveyance of mails by railway shall, subject to the provisions of this section apply in like manner as if the tramway company were a railway company, and the tramway were a railway.

(2.) The remuneration for any services performed in pursuance of this section shall be such as may be from time to time determined by agreement between the Postmaster-General and the tramway company, or, in default of agreement by the Railway and Canal Commission, and this provision shall have effect in lieu of any provisions respecting remuneration contained in the enactments relating to the conveyance of mails by railway which are applied by this section.

(3.) For the purpose of this section a requisition by the Postmaster-General may be signified by writing under the hand of any person who is at the time either Postmaster-General or a Secretary or Assistant Secretary of the Post Office, or the Inspector-General of Mails; and any document purporting to be signed by any such person as aforesaid shall, until the contrary is proved, be deemed, without proof of the official character of such person, to have been duly signed as required by this section.

III. Every tramroad authorised by any Act passed after the first day of January one thousand eight hundred and ninety-three shall, for the purposes of the conveyance of mails, be deemed to be a railway, and the enactments relating to the conveyance of mails by railway shall, subject to the provisions of this Act, apply to every such tramroad and to the company, body, or person owning or working the same as if the tramroad were a railway, and the company, body, or person were a railway company. *Carriage of mails on tramroads.*

IV. Notwithstanding anything in the Railway and Canal Traffic Act, 1888, any matter of difference directed to be determined by the Railway and Canal Commission under this Act may in the discretion of the Commission be heard and determined by the two appointed Commissioners, whose order shall be deemed to be the order of the Commission, and subject to this provision all proceedings relating to any such matter of difference shall be conducted by the Commission in the same manner as any other proceeding is conducted by them under the Railway and Canal Traffic Acts, 1873 and 1888, or any Act amending the same, and any order of the Commission upon any such difference shall be enforceable as any other order of the Commission. *Determination of differences.*

V.—(1.) In this Act—

The expression "mails" has the same meaning as in the Regulation of Railways Act, 1873, and includes parcels within the meaning of the Post Office (Parcels) Act, 1882: *Definitions. 36 & 37 Vict. c. 48. 45 & 46 Vict. c. 74.*

The expression "Act" means any Act of Parliament whether public general, local and personal, or private, and includes any order confirmed by any such Act, and a certificate granted by the Board of Trade under the Railways Construction Facilities Act, 1864, and an Order in council made by the Lord Lieutenant of Ireland under the Tramways (Ireland) Acts, 1860 to 1891, or the Railways (Ireland) Act, 1890: *27 & 28 Vict. c. 121. 53 & 54 Vict. c. 52.*

The expression "tramway" means a tramway authorised by an Act to be constructed wholly along public roads or streets without any deviation therefrom:

The expression "tramroad" means any tramroad or tramway which is not a tramway as herein-before defined, and includes a tramway or light railway constructed under the tramways

(Ireland) Acts, 1860 to 1891, or the Railways (Ireland) Act, 1890.

(2.) A railway, tramway, or tramroad shall be deemed to be authorised by an Act passed after the first day of January one thousand eight hundred and ninety-three, where the construction of the railway, tramway, or tramroad is first authorised, or where the time for its construction is extended, by an Act passed after the date aforesaid.

Short title.   VI. This Act may be cited as the Conveyance of Mails Act, 1893.

LIGHT RAILWAYS (IRELAND) ACT, 1893.
56 & 57 VICT. C. 50.
(*This Act does not extend to Scotland.*)

II.

ACT OF SEDERUNT FOR REGULATING THE PROCEDURE IN APPEALS UNDER THE RAILWAY AND CANAL TRAFFIC ACT, 1888.

EDINBURGH, 1st *June* 1889.

The Lords of Council and Session, considering that, by the Act 51 & 52 Vict. cap. 25, they are empowered to make Acts of Sederunt for regulating the procedure in appeals, authorised by said Act, from the Railway Commissioners to the Court of Session, Do hereby enact and declare that, on and after the fifteenth day of June current, the following rules shall take effect and be enforced with reference to such appeals.

I. In any case where an appeal to the Court of Session from any judgment, order, or finding of the Railway Commissioners is competent under the said Act, the same may be taken by lodging with the Registrar to the Railway Commissioners a Note of Appeal in the form, or as nearly as may be in the form, set forth in the Schedule appended hereto.

II. It shall not be competent to appeal against any judgment, order, or finding of the said Commissioners unless the Note of Appeal is lodged with the Registrar, as above provided, in the case of a final judgment within fourteen days, and in the case of any interlocutory judgment, order, or finding, within four days from the date of the judgment, order, or finding appealed against. Provided always, that the Court may, on special cause shown, allow appeals notwithstanding they have not been taken within the respective periods above provided. A final judgment, in the sense of this rule, shall mean a judgment by the Commissioners disposing of the whole question or questions raised for their determination in the proceedings in which such judgment is pronounced; and all other judgments, orders, or findings by the Commissioners shall be regarded as interlocutory.

III. The party appealing shall, within two days of lodging his Note of Appeal, intimate that he has done so to all the other parties to the proceedings in which the appeal is taken, by sending to them a copy of his Note of Appeal by registered letter.

IV. When any Note of Appeal has been lodged with the Registrar as before provided, he shall forthwith transmit the same, together with the whole pleadings and other proceedings before the Commissioners, to the Principal Clerk of that Division of the Court to which the appeal has been taken, who shall subjoin to the appeal a note of the day on which it is received.

V. The respondent in any appeal, or any party to the proceedings in which the appeal is taken, may insist in the same to the effect of having the judgment, order, or finding appealed against, altered or modified, provided that, at least three days before the appeal is heard, he shall intimate by registered letter to all parties concerned or interested in such alteration or modification, that he intends to do so, and shall intimate at same time the alteration or modification for which he intends to move.

VI. Within fourteen days after the appeal and proceedings have been received by the Principal Clerk of Session, as aforesaid, the appellant shall print and box to the Court the Note of Appeal, the judgment, order, or finding appealed against, and such other parts of the proceedings as may be necessary to be considered in disposing of the said appeal; and failing his doing so, the appeal shall be dismissed, unless the Court, or the Lord Ordinary on the Bills in time of Vacation, shall have within said fourteen days dispensed with such printing. The respondent or other party desirous of obtaining an alteration or modification of the judgment, order, or finding appealed against, as provided in Art. 5 hereof, shall, before the day on which the appeal is to be heard, lodge with the Principal Clerk, and print and box to the Court a copy of the intimation sent by him, in terms of Art. 5 hereof.

And the Lords appoint this Act to be inserted in the Books of Sederunt, and to be published in the usual manner.

JOHN INGLIS, *I.P.D.*

SCHEDULE.

The A. B. Railway Co. (or C. D., merchant in Glasgow,) appeals against the judgment (or order, or finding) of the Railway Commissioners, dated the   day of   to the Division (specify First or Second) of the Court of Session.
(Date)   (Signed by Appellant or his Law Agent.)

Or,

When a part only of the judgment, order, or finding is appealed against, the form above given shall be used, adding the words: "In so far as the said judgment (order, or finding) determines that" (specify the part of the judgment, etc., appealed against).

III.

RAILWAY AND CANAL COMMISSION RULES, 1889, AND SCHEDULE OF FORMS AND TABLE OF FEES.

General Rules made by the Commissioners established under the Statute 51 & 52 Vict. c. 25, intituled "An Act for the better regulation of Railway and Canal traffic and for other purposes," for regulating the procedure and practice before them.

Interpretation.

Interpretation of terms.

1. In the construction of these rules and the forms herein referred to, words importing the singular number shall include the plural, and words importing the plural number shall include the singular number, and the following terms shall (if not inconsistent with the context or subject matter) have the respective meanings hereinafter assigned to them; that is to say, "application" shall include complaint under the Railway and Canal Traffic Act, 1854, and the Railway and Canal Traffic Acts, 1873 and 1888; "applicant" shall include all persons or authorities authorised to make any application or complaint to the Commissioners; "defendant" shall mean the persons or company against whom the application or complaint is made, or any persons or authorities who may appear in opposition to such application or complaint; "solicitor" shall include any person entitled under section 51 of the Railway and Canal Traffic Act, 1888, to practise as an attorney or agent in

APPENDIX 83

proceedings before the Commissioners; and terms defined by the Railway and Canal Traffic Acts, 1873 and 1888, shall, unless there be something repugnant thereto in the context, have in these Rules, the same meanings that are assigned to them by those Acts.

Application or Complaint to the Commissioners.

2. Every proceeding before the Commissioners, except proceedings under section 14 of the Regulation of Railways Act, 1873, and sections 33 and 34 of the Railway and Canal Traffic Act, 1888, and applications under rules 53 and 54 of these rules, shall be commenced by an application made to them, which shall be in writing, or printed, and signed by the applicant or his solicitor, or in the case of a company or any of the authorities mentioned in section 7 of the Railway and Canal Traffic Act, 1888, being applicants, the application shall be signed by their chairman, manager, secretary, or solicitor. It shall contain a clear and concise statement of the facts, the grounds of application, and the relief or remedy to which the applicant claims to be entitled. It shall be divided into paragraphs numbered consecutively. It shall be indorsed with the name and address of the applicant, and if there be a solicitor acting for him in the matter, with the name and address of such solicitor, and if he be an agent for another solicitor in the matter, then also the name and address of such other solicitor. The application shall be according to Form No. 1 in the First Schedule hereto, or to the like effect. *Proceedings, how commenced, and form of application generally.*

3. Every application made to the Commissioners under section 6 of the Regulation of Railways Act, 1873, or section 9 of the Railway and Canal Traffic Act, 1888, shall be for an order enjoining the company complained of to do or to desist from doing the acts therein specified.

4. Every application made to the Commissioners under section 8 of the Regulation of Railways Act, 1873, shall be for an order determining the difference referred to them (with their consent) in lieu of being referred to arbitration, such consent to be signified by sealing the indorsement on such application; which indorsement shall be according to Form No. 3 in the First Schedule hereto. The applicant shall state whether or not it is a case in which any arbitrator has in any general or special Act been designated by his name or by the name of his office, or in which a standing arbitrator has been appointed under any general or special Act.

5. Every application made to the Commissioners under section 9 of the Regulation of Railways Act, 1873, shall be signed by all the parties to the difference, or their solicitors, and shall be for an order determining the difference referred to the Commissioners (with their consent). The consent of the Commissioners shall be signified as aforesaid.

6. Every application made to the Commissioners under section 10, sub-section 1, of the Regulation of Railways Act, 1873, shall be for the approval by the Commissioners of any working agreement between railway companies, whereof they desire to have the Commissioners' approval, or shall be for the exercise of any other powers (to be specified in the said application) transferred by the said sub-section to the Commissioners with respect to the approval of working agreements.[1]

7. Every application made to the Commissioners under section 25, sub-section 4, of the Railway and Canal Traffic Act, 1888, shall be for an order allowing the through rate or route, or through rate and route proposed by the applicant and objected to by the forwarding company or companies.

8. Every application made to the Commissioners under section 25, sub-sections 6 and 7, of the Railway and Canal Traffic Act, 1888, shall be for an order allowing or determining (as the case may be), the apportionment of the through rate objected to by the forwarding company or companies.

9. Every application made to the Commissioners under section 14 of the Regulation of Railways Act, 1873, and under sections 33 and 34 of the Railway and Canal Traffic Act, 1888, may be by summons, and shall be for an order upon the company, against whom the application is made to keep at the stations, wharves, or ports named in such summons, a book or books of rates and distances, and other particulars required by those sections or either of them, or for an order allowing inspection of such books, or for an order to distinguish in the book or books in such summons mentioned, how much of the rate in respect whereof the application is made, is for the conveyance of the particular description of traffic therein named on the railway or canal in question, including therein tolls for the use of the railway or canal, for use of carriages or vessels, or for locomotive or other tractive power,

---

[1] The public notice required to be given by the railway companies should be according to Form No. 9 of Schedule I., and the Commissioners' directions prescribing the steps to be taken to obtain their approval of working agreements are set out in Schedule IV.

and how much is for other expenses, specifying the nature and detail of such other expenses. The applicant in such last-mentioned case shall file an affidavit at the time of taking out such summons, stating that he is interested in the matter, and showing how he is interested therein.

10. Every application made to the Commissioners under section 15 of the Regulation of Railways Act, 1873, or under section 37 of the Railway and Canal Traffic Act, 1888, shall be for them to hear and determine the question or dispute therein mentioned, with respect to the terminal charges of the company against whom the application is made, and to decide what is a reasonable sum to be paid to such company in respect of such terminal charges.

11. Every application made to the Commissioners under section 16 of the Regulation of Railways Act, 1873, shall be for them to sanction the agreement therein mentioned, such sanction to be signified by certificate under their seal. Before the companies enter into such agreement, notice of their intention to do so shall be given by them, or one of them, by advertisement to be inserted once at least in each of three successive weeks, in some newspaper published or circulating in the county or counties, in which the canal to which the proposed agreement relates, or some portion of such canal is situate. Such notice shall be according to Form No. 8 in the First Schedule hereto.

12. Every application made to the Commissioners under section 17 of the Regulation of Railways Act, 1873, shall be for an order upon the railway company, against whom the application is made, restraining them from permitting and suffering the canal therein mentioned, or parts thereof, or works belonging thereto, to remain unrepaired, or in want of dredging, or not in good working condition, or without proper supplies of water thereto; and also enjoining them to keep and maintain the said canal or such parts thereof, or such works thereto belonging, thoroughly repaired or dredged or in good working condition, or to preserve the supplies of water to the same. The application in such case shall specify the obstruction, want of repair, or other defect sought to be remedied, and show in what part of the canal or works such obstruction, want of repair, or other defect exists.

13. Every application made to the Commissioners under section 10 of the Railway and Canal Traffic Act, 1888, shall be for them to hear and determine the question or dispute therein mentioned with respect to the legality of any toll, rate, or charge or portion of a toll, rate or charge charged, or sought to be

charged by any company for merchandise traffic. The parties may concur in stating such question or dispute in the form of a joint application without further pleadings.

14. Every application by a company under section 20, sub-section 3, of the Railway and Canal Traffic Act, 1888, shall be for an order determining whether the group rate, or the rate as to which there is a doubt, is or is not a contravention of section 2 of the Railway and Canal Traffic Act, 1854, and in any such application, the company applying shall state the nature of the doubt considered to exist.

Where such an application is in respect of a group rate it shall specify, in addition to the amount of the rate, the names of the places grouped together, and such distances as may be material for the purposes of the application.

The company making the application for such order, shall give one month's public notice of their intention to apply to the Commissioners under this section, by advertisement in at least one London daily newspaper, and in one newspaper in general circulation in the district or districts within which the group is comprehended; such advertisements shall in each case be inserted in each of three successive weeks, at intervals of not less than a week, in each of the newspapers in which they appear. In such notice full particulars shall be given of the group rate, or the rate or rates as to which the Commissioners' determination is to be asked.

15. Every application to the Commissioners under section 38, sub-section 1, of the Railway and Canal Traffic Act, 1888, shall be for an order on the railway company, or on the directors or officers of the railway company, or on any person acting on their behalf, and having such control or right of interference as mentioned in the said section, requiring the tolls, rates, and charges levied by such railway company, directors, officers, or persons on the traffic of, or for the conveyance of merchandise on, the canal in respect of which the complaint is made to be altered and adjusted in such a manner, that the same shall be reasonable as compared with the rates and charges for the conveyance of merchandise on the railway. The applicant shall state in what manner the existing tolls, rates, and charges so levied as aforesaid, are calculated to divert traffic from the canal to the railway to the detriment of the canal, or of persons sending traffic over the canal or other canals adjacent to it, and shall state the amount and the particulars of the alteration or reduction proposed.

16. The procedure in cases under the following Acts shall be in each case, as nearly as may be, the same as that directed to be taken by Rule 4 of these rules, in proceedings under the 8th section of the Regulation of Railways Act, 1873.

(*a.*) Differences between the Postmaster-General and any company, referred to the Commissioners under the provisions of section 19 of the Regulation of Railways Act, 1873. —*Differences under sect. 19 of Regulation of Railways Act, 1873, the*

(*b.*) Differences referred to the decision of the Commissioners by the Board of Trade under the provisions of Part 2 of the Board of Trade Arbitrations Act, 1874. —*Board of Trade Arbitrations Act, 1874; and the Tele-*

(*c.*) Differences required by sections 4 and 5 of the Telegraph Act, 1878, to be referred to the decision of the Commissioners. —*graph Act, 1878.*

17. When the Board of Trade, under the provisions of section 3 of the Cheap Trains Act, 1883, have referred any matters contained in the said section for the decision of the Commissioners, the railway company or companies concerned shall, on receiving notice from the commissioners to do so, file an answer within such time as the Commissioners may order, to the allegations contained in the order of the Board of Trade referring the matter as aforesaid. —*Reference under Cheap Trains Act, 1883.*

Claim for Damages.

18. If the applicant, in any matter which the Commissioners have jurisdiction to hear and determine, claims damages from the defendant, he shall in such case state in his application the amount of damages claimed, and the matter in respect of which such claim is made, and the defendant may before or at the time of delivering his answer, or, by leave of the Commissioners, at any later time, pay into court a sum of money by way of satisfaction, which shall be taken to admit the matter in respect of which the payment is made; or the defendant may, with an answer denying liability, pay money into court. If the defendant, in any matter which the Commissioners have jurisdiction to hear and determine, desire to have all claims for damages in respect of such matter dealt with by the Commissioners, he shall make such claim in his answer, or, by leave of the Commissioners, at any subsequent stage of the proceedings. —*Damages, how claimed.*

The provisions of rules 2, 3, 4, 5, 6, and 7 of Order 22 of the Rules of the Supreme Court, 1883, and the forms required to be used in such rules shall, *mutatis mutandis*, apply to and be used in all proceedings in this rule provided for.[1]

---
[1] The provisions of the rules and the forms referred to are set in Schedule II.

Money paid into court in applications made to the Commissioners in English cases, shall be paid into the Bank of England (Law Courts Branch), and the manner of payment into and out of court, and the manner in which money in court shall be dealt with, shall be subject to the regulations contained in the Supreme Court Funds Rules, in force for the time being so far as the same are applicable.

Money paid into court on applications made to the Commissioners in Scotch cases, shall be paid into one of the incorporated or chartered banks in Scotland.

Money paid into court on applications made to the Commissioners in Irish cases shall be paid into the Bank of Ireland.

Filing Application.

Filing application at the Commissioners' office.

19. Every application to which any of the foregoing rules apply shall be indorsed as required by Rule 2, and filed with the Registrar to the Commissioners (herein-after in these rules called "the Registrar") at their office, and except in cases under sections 10 and 16 of the Regulation of Railways Act, 1873, three copies of the application shall also be left with the Registrar. The Registrar shall make out a list of the applications so filed according to the order in which they are received by him, and such list may be inspected at the office during office hours. The applications shall be heard by the Commissioners so far as it may in their judgment be practicable, according to the order in which they are so entered upon the list.

Indorsement on Application.

Indorsement upon application.

20. In all proceedings (except proceedings under sections 8, 9, 10, and 19 of the Regulation of Railways Act, 1873, and subject to Rule 22 of these rules) a copy of the application shall be indorsed, with a notice to the defendant to put in an answer to the application within fifteen days from the service thereof, and that in default of such answer being put in within the time named, or any extension thereof duly granted, the Commissioners may proceed to hear the said application *ex parte*. Such indorsement shall be according to Form No. 2 in the First Schedule hereto, and shall be sealed by the Registrar with their seal.

Service of Application.

Service of application.

21. A copy of the application indorsed as aforesaid shall in all cases (except under sections 9 and 10 of the Regulation of Railways

Act, 1873, and subject to Rule 22 of these rules) be served by leaving the same with the manager, secretary, or chief clerk of the defendant at his principal office in any part of the United Kingdom, or in such manner as the Commissioners by special order may direct, but no such personal service shall be necessary when the defendant's solicitor or agent undertakes in writing to accept service of such copy on his behalf.

Suspension of Proceedings.

22. If the Commissioners think fit, in pursuance of section 7 of the Regulation of Railways Act, 1873, to communicate an application to the company against whom it is made, so as to afford them an opportunity of making observations thereon before requiring or permitting any formal proceedings to be taken thereon, they shall give notice thereof to the applicant within seven days from the date of the application having been left at their office, and thereupon all formal proceedings thereon shall be suspended until further notice from the Commissioners to the applicant. Communication by Commissioners to missioners to company complained of.

23. The Commissioners may also within the said period of seven days, or at any time thereafter, require further information or particulars or documents from the applicant, and may suspend all formal proceedings upon the application until satisfied in this respect. Commissioners requiring further information.

24. If the Commissioners at any stage of the proceedings think fit to direct inquiries to be made under section 3 of the Railway and Canal Traffic Act, 1854, they shall give notice thereof to the parties to the application, and may stay proceedings, or any part of the proceedings thereon, until further notice from the Commissioners. Inquiries under the Act of 1854.

Consent Cases.

25. In all cases the parties may, by consent in writing, dispense with the formal proceedings herein-after mentioned, or some portion of them, and orders by consent may be drawn up, and, if approved of by the Commissioners, may be sealed with their seal. Parties dispensing with formal proceedings.

Answer.

26. Within 15 days from the service of the application, or within such shorter or extended time as may be fixed by the Commissioners, the defendant shall file, with the registrar, their answer to the application, and leave with him three copies of the same, and the defendant shall, within such time, deliver to the applicant or to his solicitor a signed copy of the answer. The Form of, and time for filing and delivery.

answer shall contain a clear and concise statement of the facts which form the ground of defence, or of any other objections relied upon. It may admit the whole or any part of the facts stated in the application. It shall be divided into paragraphs numbered consecutively, and it shall be signed by the person actually making the same, and who is acquainted with the facts stated therein. It shall be indorsed with the name and address of the defendant, and if there be a solicitor acting for him in the matter, with the name and address of such solicitor, and if he be an agent for another solicitor in the matter, then also with the name and address of such other solicitor. It shall be according to Form No. 4 in the First Schedule hereto, or to the like effect.

Reply.

Form of, and time for filing and delivery.
27. Within six days from the delivery of the answer to the applicant, or within such shorter or extended time as may be fixed by any special order of the Commissioners, the applicant shall file his reply (if any) with the Registrar, and leave with him three copies of the same, and shall within such time deliver to the defendant or to his solicitor a copy of the reply. The applicant, in such reply, may object to the said answer as being insufficient, stating the grounds of such objection, or deny the facts stated therein, or may admit the whole or any part of such facts. The reply shall be signed by the applicant, his solicitor, or agent, and be according to Form No. 5 in the First Schedule hereto, or to the like effect.

Pleadings after Reply by Leave.

Pleadings after reply.
28. No pleading subsequent to reply other than a joinder of issue shall be pleaded without leave of the Commissioners.

Close of Pleadings by implied Joinder.

Close of pleadings on default.
29. If the applicant does not deliver a reply, or any party does not deliver any subsequent pleading within the period allowed for that purpose, the pleadings shall be deemed to be closed at the expiration of that period, and all material statements of facts in the pleading last delivered shall be deemed to have been denied and put in issue.

Power to direct and settle Issues.

Commissioners may direct issues.
30. If it appear to the Commissioners at any time that the statements in the application or answer, or reply, do not sufficiently raise or disclose the issues of fact in dispute between the parties,

they may direct them to prepare issues, and such issues shall, if the parties differ, be settled by the Commissioners.

Preliminary Questions of Law.

31. The Commissioners may, by consent of the parties to any proceedings before them, or on the application of either party, order any point of law raised by the pleading to be set down for hearing and disposed of at any time before the hearing of the application. The argument of such point of law shall take place before not less than three Commissioners, and upon such hearing, if, in the opinion of the Commissioners, the decision of such point of law substantially disposes of the whole application, the Commissioners may order that the argument shall be the hearing of the case, and thereupon may grant and dismiss the application or make such other order therein as may seem to them just. Commissioners may decide preliminary questions of law.

Preliminary Meeting.

32 If it appear to the Commissioners at any time before the hearing of the application that it will be to the advantage of the parties to hold a preliminary meeting for the purpose of fixing or altering the place of hearing, determining the mode of conducting the inquiry, the admitting of certain facts, or the proof of them by affidavit, or for any other purpose, they shall have power to hold such meeting upon giving notice thereof to the parties, and may thereupon make such order as shall seem to them fit under the circumstances. Commissioners may hold preliminary meeting.

Preliminary Communication with the Parties.

33. The Commissioners may, if they think fit, instead of holding such meeting as in the preceding rule mentioned, communicate with the parties in writing, and may require answers to such inquiries as they may think fit to make. Commissioners may communicate with parties.

Interim Injunction.

34. An interim injunction may be moved for at any stage of the proceedings. Such application (except as after provided) shall be made to and be disposed of by the *ex officio* Commissioner for the part of the United Kingdom in which the proceedings (under which the application is made) are depending. Notice of such application shall be given to the parties affected thereby at least two clear days before the application is moved: Provided that in cases of emergency it shall be competent to the *ex officio* Commissioner to grant the interim injunction sought without previous notice. An applica- Commissioners may grant interim injunction.

tion to dissolve any injunction may be made at any time to the *ex officio* Commissioner on two clear days' notice to the party in whose favour the injunction was granted.

Discovery of Documents and Interrogatories.

Applications for discovery.

35. In England and Ireland either party may, without filing any affidavit, apply to the Commissioners for an order to direct the other party to make discovery on oath of the documents which are or have been in his possession or power relating to the matter in question. In Scotland either party may apply to the *ex officio* Commissioner for an order on the other party to produce all documents which are in his possession or power relating to the matter in question, or either party may apply as aforesaid for a diligence to recover all documents, in whosesoever possession they may be, relating to the matter in question. Provided that, in either case, the party making the application shall give to the other party at least three days' notice of his intention to make it, and shall (where a diligence is sought), with such notice, furnish a copy of the specification setting forth the documents for recovery of which a diligence is sought.

36. In England and Ireland the applicant may, at any time after serving his application, and the defendant may, at or after the time of delivering his answer, by leave of the Commissioners, deliver interrogatories in writing for the examination of the opposite party.

Interrogatories shall be answered by affidavit to be filed within ten days or within such other time as the Commissioners may allow. The interrogatories may be answered partly by one person and partly by another or others, but in all cases the party answering any part thereof shall state in his answer that the matters stated by him are within his personal knowledge, and if any person interrogated omits to answer, or answers insufficiently, the party interrogating may apply to the Commissioners for an order requiring him to answer, or to answer further, as the case may be.

No payment into court of a sum of money as deposit shall be required from a party seeking discovery by interrogatories or otherwise.

In Scotland either of the parties may at any time after the service of the application or lodging of the answer respectively, and before any proof has been adduced, present to the *ex officio* Commissioner a statement of facts which he desires to be answered by his opponent, and may move the *ex officio* Commissioner for an order on his opponent to answer the same, with which motion the *ex officio* Commissioner shall deal as appears just. Notice of such motion (accompanied by a copy of the statement of facts) to be served at least three days before the motion is to be heard.

Production and Inspection of Documents.

37. It shall be lawful for the Commissioners, at any time during the pendency of any matter before them, to order the production by any party thereto, upon oath, of such of the documents in his possession or power relating to any such matter as the Commissioners shall think right; and the Commissioners may deal with such documents, when produced before them, in such manner as shall appear just. Production of documents on oath.

38. Either party shall be entitled at any time before or at the hearing of the case, to give a notice in writing to the other party in whose application or answer or reply, reference is made to any document, to produce it for the inspection of the party giving such notice, or of his solicitor, and to permit him to take copies thereof, and any party not complying with such notice shall not afterwards be at liberty to put any such document in evidence on his behalf in such proceeding, without the leave of the Commissioners, unless he satisfy the Commissioners that he had sufficient cause for not complying with such notice. Documents referred to in pleadings.

Notice to produce.

39. Either party may give to the other a notice in writing to produce such documents as relate to any matters in difference (specifying the said documents), and which are in the possession or control of such other party, and if such notice be not complied with, secondary evidence of the contents of the said documents may be given by or on behalf of the party who gave such notice. Notice to produce.

Notice to admit.

40. Either party may give to the other party a notice in writing to admit any documents saving all just exceptions, and in case of neglect or refusal to admit after such notice, the costs of proving such documents shall be paid by the party so neglecting or refusing, whatever the result of the application may be, unless at the hearing the Commissioners certify that the refusal to admit was reasonable, and no costs of proving any document shall be allowed unless such notice be given, except where the omission to Notice to admit.

give the notice is, in the opinion of the taxing officer, a saving of expense.

Notice of Discontinuance.

Notice where application withdrawn or settled.

41. When any application made to the Commissioners has been withdrawn or settled, the applicant shall immediately thereupon give notice thereof to the Registrar.

Witnesses.

Attendance of witnesses.

42. The attendance of witnesses, with or without documents, shall be enforced by subpœna which may be sued out by either party requiring the attendance of such witness. Such subpœna shall be according to Forms No. 6 or 7 in the First Schedule hereto, and shall be sealed by the Registrar with the seal of the Commission, and may be served in any part of the United Kingdom. The witnesses shall be entitled to the same protection as when subpœnaed or cited to attend a superior court, and the laws and practice in force for the time being relating to witnesses in a superior court, shall apply to them in proceedings before the Commissioners.

Appointing Date of Hearing.

Application to fix date of hearing.

43. The applicant, at the time of filing his reply (if any), or if the defendant make default in putting in his answer, or at any time after the pleadings are closed, may apply to the Registrar to fix a date for the hearing. If the applicant does not within six weeks after the close of the pleadings, or within such extended time as the Commissioners may allow, apply to the Registrar to fix a date for the hearing, the defendant may do so. No such application shall be made without two days' previous notice in writing to the opposite party. If either of the parties fail to appear on the application to fix a day for hearing, notice of the day appointed shall be served within a time to be named by the Registrar.

Depositing maps, plans, etc.

The parties shall leave with the Registrar, six days before the day fixed for the hearing, any maps, plans, time-tables, and special Acts or other documents referred to in the application, answer, reply, or other pleading, or which may be useful in explaining or supporting the same.

The Hearing.

Power of Commissioners to proceed ex parte.

44. If the applicant does not appear at the time and place appointed for the hearing, the Commissioners may dismiss the

application, and if the defendant does not appear at such time and place, and the Commissioners are satisfied that the notice of the hearing was duly served, they may hear and determine the application *ex parte*, and if at any adjournment of the hearing the parties or either of them do not appear, the Commissioners may decide the case in their absence.

Evidence at the Hearing.

45. The witnesses at the hearing shall be examined *vivâ voce*, but the Commissioners may at any time, and whether before or at the hearing, for sufficient reason, order that any particular facts may be proved by affidavit, or that the affidavit of any witness may be read at the hearing on such conditions as they may think reasonable, or that any witness whose attendance ought for some sufficient cause to be dispensed with, be examined by interrogatories or otherwise before a person to be appointed by them for that purpose, provided that when it appears to the Commissioners that the other party *bonâ fide* desires the production of a witness for cross-examination, and that such witness can be produced, an order shall not be made authorising the evidence of such witness to be given by affidavit. *To be vivâ voce except in certain cases, and whether before or at the hearing.*

Depositions taken before a person authorised to take them may be read at the hearing without calling the deponents unless the Commissioners otherwise order.

46. The Commissioners may require further evidence to be given either *vivâ voce*, or by affidavit, or by deposition taken before a person appointed by them for that purpose. *Commissioners may require further evidence.*

47. The hearing of the case, when once commenced, shall proceed, so far as in the judgment of the Commissioners may be practicable and convenient, from day to day. *Hearing to proceed from day to day.*

View.

48. In any case in which, in the opinion of the Commissioners, a view is necessary or desirable, it may be had by one or more Commissioners as they may direct. *Power of Commissioners to view.*

Judgment of Commissioners.

49. After hearing the case the Commissioners may dismiss the application, or make an order thereon in favour of the defendants, or reserve their decision, or make such other order upon the application as may be warranted by the evidence, and may seem to them just. *Judgment of Commissioners.*

May be in writing and sent or delivered to the parties.

50. The Commissioners may give their decision in writing, signed by them, and it may be sent or delivered to the respective parties, and it shall not be necessary to hold a court merely for the purpose of giving such decision.

Taxation of Costs.

Costs, how taxed.

51. Costs shall be taxed upon the order of the Commissioners under which they are payable, and such costs shall, if required, be taxed by the Registrar or such other person as the Commissioner may direct.

Alteration or Rescission of Order.

Alteration or rescission of orders.

52. Any application to the Commissioners to review and rescind or vary any decision or order previously made by them, and not being a decision or order upon an interlocutory application, nor under Rule 14 of these rules, shall be made within 28 days after the said decision or order shall have been communicated to the parties, unless the Commissioners think fit to enlarge the time for making such application.

Any application to the Commissioners to review and rescind or vary any decision or order previously made by them upon an interlocutory application, shall be made within four days after the said decision or order shall have been communicated to the parties, unless the Commissioners think fit to enlarge the time for making such application.

Every application under this rule shall be made by motion; and no such motion shall be made without two clear days' previous notice in writing to the Registrar and to the parties affected thereby.

Interlocutory Applications.

Interlocutory applications.

53. Where not otherwise provided for in these rules, all interlocutory applications shall, unless otherwise specially ordered, be heard by the Registrar upon summons duly served, and may be determined in a summary way. Such application may, if the Registrar thinks fit, be adjourned, either before or at the time of hearing before him, into court for hearing before the Commissioners.

Any person affected by any order or decision of the Registrar in any matter involving questions of law, may appeal therefrom to the *ex officio* Commissioner, and in any other matter to the Com-

missioners. Such appeal shall be by way of indorsement on the
summons by the Registrar at the request of any party or by
notice in writing to attend before the Commissioners without a
fresh summons. Such notice shall be given to the Registrar and
to the opposite party within four days after the decision complained of, or such further time as may be allowed by the
Registrar or by the *ex officio* Commissioner, or the Commissioners.

An appeal from the Registrar's decision shall be no stay of
proceedings unless so ordered by the Registrar or by the *ex officio*
Commissioner, or the Commissioners.

Affidavits.

54. Affidavits shall be confined to such facts as the witness is — Affidavits,
able of his own knowledge to prove, except on interlocutory pro- how framed.
ceedings, on which statements as to his belief with the grounds
thereof may be admitted. The costs of every affidavit which
shall unnecessarily set forth matters of hearsay or argumentative
matter or copies of or extracts from documents shall be paid by
the party using or filing the same.

55. Any affidavit used in any proceeding before the Commis- — Before whom
missioners may be sworn as follows : sworn.

In the United Kingdom before any of the said Commissioners
or the Registrar, or the officer appointed by the Commissioners to
administer oaths in proceedings before them (and in these cases
without the payment of any fee), or before a person authorised to
administer oaths in any of the superior courts, or before a commissioner empowered to take or receive affidavits, or before a justice
of the peace for the county or place where it is sworn or made.

In Scotland, in addition to the above-mentioned persons, before
any sheriff-depute or his substitute or a justice of the peace.

In any place in the British dominions out of the United
Kingdom, before any court, judge, or justice of the peace, or any
person authorised to administer oaths there in any court.

In any place out of the British dominions, before a British
minister, consul, or vice-consul.

The Commissioners shall take judicial notice of the seal or
signature, as the case may be, of any such court, judge, minister,
consul, or vice-consul attached, appended, or subscribed to any
such affidavit.

56. Affidavits used in any proceedings before the Commis- — Filing of,
sioners shall be filed in their office, and office copies of the same and giving
office copies
of, and of
other docu-
ments.

and of other documents filed in their office may be procured by the parties on application to the Registrar.

Computation of Time.

Time, how computed.

57. In all cases in which any particular number of days, not expressed to be clear days, is prescribed by the Railway and Canal Traffic Acts, 1873 and 1888, or by these rules, the same shall be reckoned exclusively of the first day and inclusively of the last day, unless the last day shall happen to fall on a Sunday, Christmas Day, or Good Friday, or a day appointed for a public fast or thanksgiving, in which case the time shall be reckoned exclusively of that day also.

What days to be excluded.

58. The days between Thursday next before and the Wednesday next after Easter Day, and the day appointed to be kept as the Queen's Birthday, and Whit Monday and Whit Tuesday, and Christmas Day, and the three following days, shall not be reckoned or included in any proceedings under the Railway and Canal Traffic Acts, 1873 and 1888.

Pleadings in the vacations.

59. The time between the 12th day of August and the 24th day of October in England and Ireland, and in Scotland between the 20th day of March and the 12th day of May, and between the 20th day of July and the 15th day of October, shall be reckoned in the computation of the times appointed or allowed by these rules for filing, amending, or delivering, unless otherwise ordered.

Registrar's Office, when open.

Registrar's Office, when open.

60. The Registrar's office shall be open daily from 10 o'clock in the forenoon till 4 o'clock in the afternoon, or till such later time as the Commissioners may direct, except upon Saturday, when it shall be open from 10 o'clock in the forenoon till 2 o'clock in the afternoon, and except between the 12th day of August and the 24th day of October, when the Office is to be open from 11 o'clock in the forenoon till 1 o'clock in the afternoon.

The office shall be closed on the following days, namely, Good Friday, Easter Eve, Monday and Tuesday in Easter week, Christmas Day and the three following days, and the day appointed to be kept as the Queen's Birthday, and Whit Monday and Whit Tuesday.

Sittings of the Court.

Vacations.

61. Every *ex officio* Commissioner shall be entitled to the same vacations as are observed in the superior court of which he is a

member. During the periods observed as vacations in the Superior Courts the Lord Chancellor in England, the Lord President of the Court of Session in Scotland, and the Lord Chancellor in Ireland, may appoint any Judge of a Superior Court to take the place and perform the whole functions of the *ex officio* Commissioner for these parts of the United Kingdom respectively, in case of the *ex officio* Commissioner being absent or temporarily unable to fulfil his duties.

Adjournment.

62. The Commisssioners may from time to time adjourn any proceedings before them.   *Power of Commissioners to adjourn.*

Amendment.

63. The Commissioners may at any stage of the proceedings allow any pleadings to be amended, or may order to be struck out any matters which may tend to prejudice, embarrass, or delay the fair hearing of the case, and all such amendments shall be made as may be necessary for the purpose of determining the real questions in controversy between the parties.   *Power of Commissioners to amend.*

Formal Objections.

64. No proceedings before the Commissioners shall be defeated by any formal objection.   *Formal objections not to prevail.*

Practice of Superior Courts, when applicable.

65. The general principles of practice in the superior courts may be adopted and applied at the discretion of the Commissioners to proceedings before them.   *Discretion of Commissioners in cases not expressly provided for.*

Where, in any complaint or other proceeding before the Commissioners, the defendant has his domicile or principal place of business or head office in England, such proceedings shall be deemed to be proceedings falling to be dealt with by the *ex officio* Commissioner for England, in so far as he is, by statute or any Rule of Court, charged with any duty in connexion therewith, and in like manner, where the defendant has his domicile or principal place of business or head office in Scotland or Ireland, the proceedings shall be dealt with by the *ex officio* Commissioners for Scotland and Ireland respectively. Where there are in any proceedings more defendants than one having their domicile or principal place of business or head office in different parts of the

United Kingdom, the Commissioners shall determine before which of the *ex officio* Commissioners such proceedings shall depend.

Subject to this rule, if any question should arise whether the Superior Court of England, Ireland, or Scotland is the court with reference to which in the particular case the expression "superior court" in any of the said rules is to be understood, the same shall be determined by the Commissioners, who shall make such order in that behalf as they shall think right under the circumstances, either with reference to the particular matter under consideration only or with reference to the future conduct of the proceedings in general, or any of them, or with reference to anything that has already been done.

Provided that if any steps or proceedings have been taken under the practice of one superior court, and the Commissioners shall think that the practice of any other superior court ought to be applied, they shall make such order as shall, as far as practicable, and as is just under the circumstances, prevent the steps already taken from being rendered nugatory, and any expense already incurred from being thrown away.

Enlargement or Abridgement of Time.

Power to enlarge or abridge time.

66. The Commissioners or the Registrar, subject to an appeal to the Commissioners, may enlarge or abridge the time appointed by these rules, or fixed by any order, for doing any act or taking any proceeding upon such terms, if any, as the justice of the case may require, and any such enlargement may be ordered, although the application for the same is not made until after the expiration of the time appointed or allowed.

Enlarging time by consent.

The time for delivering, amending, or filing any answer, reply, or other pleading or document may be enlarged by consent in writing, without application to the Commissioners. Such written consent shall be left with the Registrar at the time of filing the answer, reply, or other pleading or document.

Transmission of Documents and Fees by Post.

Documents, etc., sent by post.

67. Where an applicant does not reside in London, and he has no solicitor or agent there, all pleadings and documents required by these rules to be sealed, filed in, or delivered at the Commissioners' office, may be sent by post, addressed to "The Registrar of the Court of the Railway and Canal Commission," and the fees payable (if any) in respect thereof may be sent by post, by post-office order, payable to "The Registrar of the Railway and Canal

Commission," to the Registrar, who shall cause stamps to be procured to the amount of such remittances, and such stamps to be obliterated. All letters, notices, or documents sent by post to the officers of the Commission shall be prepaid.

Table of Fees.

68. The fees, a table whereof is in the Third Schedule hereunto annexed, may be demanded and taken in respect of the proceedings before the Commissioners. *What fees may be taken.*

Signed the 22nd day of February 1889.

ALFRED WILLS.
JOHN TRAYNER.
JAMES MURPHY.
F. PEEL.
WM. P. PRICE.

Approved,
    HALSBURY, C.

Approved,
    M. E. HICKS-BEACH,
        President of the Board of Trade.

SCHEDULES.

FIRST SCHEDULE.

FORMS.

No. 1. Application.
No. 2. Indorsement.
No. 3. Indorsement required by Rule 4.
No. 4. Answer.
No. 5. Reply.
No. 6. Form of Subpœna *ad testificandum*.
No. 7. Form of Subpœna *duces tecum*.
No. 8. Notice required by Rule 11.
No. 9. Form of Notice to the public required to be given by Railway Companies by section 24 of Railway Clauses Act, 1863.

The forms of proceedings contained in this Schedule may be used in the cases to which they are applicable, with such alterations as the circumstances of the case may render necessary, but any variance therefrom, not being in matter of substance, shall not affect their validity or regularity.

No. 1.

Application.

In the Court of the Railway and Canal Commission.

In the matter of the application of *A.B.* against The Company. } *A.B.* states that
1.
2.

And the said *A.B.* applies to the said court under the above-mentioned Acts for an order enjoining the said Company [*here state concisely the nature of the application, as for example,*] to desist from giving any undue preference to themselves or other persons in the carrying or in the collecting, carrying, and delivering, for themselves or other persons, of goods and parcels, or in their charges for the same over the said *A.B.* in the carrying of such goods and parcels for him, and enjoining the said Company not to subject him to any undue prejudice in respect thereof.

Dated this   day of   18

(Signed), *A.B.*

or

C.D.

Solicitor for the Applicant.

No. 2.

Indorsement on application.

To the within named   Company.

You are hereby commanded by the Court of the Railway and Canal Commission within 15 days from the service of the within application to put in your answer to the same, and take notice that in default of such answer being put in within such time or any extension thereof duly granted, the said Court may proceed to hear the said application *ex parte*.

(Sealed.)

APPENDIX

[*Indorsement.*]

The within application is made by *A.B.* of
(*stating address and occupation, and if there be a solicitor in the matter*)
by *C.D.* of   (*and if he be agent for the solicitor*)
as agent for *E.F.* of   solicitor for the said
A.B., and was filed on the   day of
18

No. 3.

Indorsement required by Rule 4.

To the within named   Company.

Take notice that the Court of the Railway and Canal Commission, having consented to the within-mentioned difference (or differences) being referred to it for its decision in lieu of being referred to arbitration, you are hereby commanded within   days from the service upon you of the within statement to put in your answer to the same, and take notice, that in default of such answer being put in within such time, or any extension thereof duly granted, the said Court may proceed to hear and determine the said difference *ex parte*.

(Sealed.)

No. 4.

Answer.

In the Court of the Railway and Canal Commission.

In the matter
of the application of *A.B.*
against
The   Company.

{ The   Company in answer to the Application of *A.B.* state that—
1.
2.
This Answer is made on behalf of the said Company by *C.D.* of   , who is acquainted with the facts stated therein.

Dated this   day of   18 .

(Signed.)

No. 5.

Reply.

In the Court of the Railway and Canal Commission.

In the matter of the application of *A.B.* against The   company. { The said *A.B.* in reply to the answer of the said   Company states that—
1.
2. And the said *A.B.* admits that

Dated this   day of   18 .
(Signed)   *A.B.*
or
C.D.
Solicitor for the said Applicant.

No. 6.

Subpœna ad Testificandum.

In the Court of the Railway and Canal Commission.

In the matter of the application of *A.B.*, Applicant,
against
The   Company, Defendant.

Victoria, by the grace of God, &c., to [*the names of three witnesses may be inserted*], greeting. We command you to attend before the Railway and Canal Commissioners at
on   day the   day, of   18 ,
at the hour of   in the   noon, and so from day to day until the above application is tried, to give evidence on behalf of the applicant (or defendant).

Witness, &c.

No. 7.

Subpœna Duces Tecum.

In the Court of the Railway and Canal Commission.

In the Matter of the Application of *A.B.*, Applicant,
against
The   Company, Defendant.

Victoria, by the Grace of God, &c., to [*the names of three witnesses may be inserted*], greeting. We command you to attend before the Railway and Canal Commissioners at   , on   day, the   day of   18 , at the hour

of   in the   noon, and so from day to day until the above application is tried, to give evidence on behalf of the applicant (or defendant), and also to bring with you and produce at the aforesaid time and place [*specify documents to be produced*].
Witness.

No. 8.
Notice required by Rule 11.
The Railway and Canal Traffic Acts, 1873 and 1888.

Notice is hereby given that it is the intention of the   Railway Company and the   Canal Company, subject to the sanction of the Railway and Canal Commissioners, to enter into an agreement for the following purposes, viz. (among other things), the

and that a copy of the proposed agreement can be seen at the office of the Railway and Canal Commission at
Dated this   day of   18 .
Secretary to the
(Solicitor or agent)

No. 9.
Form of Notice to be given to the Public by Railway Companies of their intention to enter into Agreements amongst themselves under Part III. of the Railway Clauses Act, 1863.

Notice is hereby given pursuant to the provisions of the Railways Clauses Act, 1863, and the Railway and Canal Traffic Acts, 1873 and 1888, and the   Act, 18 , that it is the intention of the   Railway Company and the   Railway Company to enter into an agreement for the following purposes, viz. (among other things), the
and that any company or person aggrieved by such proposed agreement and desiring to object thereto, may bring such objection before the Railway and Canal Commissioners by sending the same in writing, addressed to the Registrar to the Railway and Canal Commissioners, at their office, at the
London, on or before the [1]   day of

---

[1] 28 days should intervene between the date of the newspaper containing the first insertion of this notice and the date here inserted. See Schedule IV.

18   , in which office a copy of the proposed agreement can be seen.

Dated this   day of   18
              Secretary to the
              (Solicitor or agent)

SECOND SCHEDULE.

Rules 2, 3, 4, 5, 6, 7 of Order XXII. of the Rules of the Supreme Court, 1883, referred to in Rule 18 of these Rules.

2. Payment into court shall be signified in the defence, and the claim or cause of action in satisfaction of which such payment is made shall be specified therein.

3. With a defence setting up a tender before action, the sum of money alleged to have been tendered must be brought into court.

4. If the defendant pays money into court before delivering his defence, he shall serve upon the plaintiff a notice specifying both the fact that he has paid in such money, and also the claim or cause of action in respect of which such payment has been made. Such notice shall be in the form No. 3 in Appendix B., with such variations as circumstances may require.

[Form No. 3, referred to in the foregoing rule.]

Heading as in form.[1]

Take notice that the defendant has paid into court   *l*., and says that that sum is enough to satisfy the plaintiff's claim [*or* the plaintiff's claim for, etc.]

                        Z., defendant's solicitor.
To Mr. X. Y., the plaintiff's solicitor.

5. In the following cases of payment into court under this order, viz. :—

(*a*.) When payment into court is made before delivery of defence ;

(*b*.) When the liability of the defendant in respect of the claim or cause of action in satisfaction of which the payment into court is made is not denied in the defence ;

(*c*.) When payment into court is made with a defence setting up a tender of the sum paid ;

the money paid into court shall be paid out to the plaintiff on his

---

[1] NOTE.—In proceedings before the Commissioners the heading of this form will be the same as the heading of the forms in the First Schedule.

request, or to his solicitor, on the plaintiff's written authority, unless the court or a judge shall otherwise order.

6. When the liability of the defendant in respect of the claim or cause of action, in satisfaction of which the payment into court has been made, is denied in the defence, the following rules shall apply:—

(*a*.) The plaintiff may accept, in satisfaction of the claim or cause of action in respect of which the payment into court has been made, the sum so paid in, in which case he shall be entitled to have the money paid out to him as hereinafter provided, notwithstanding the defendant's denial of liability, whereupon all further proceedings in respect of such claim or cause of action, except as to costs, shall be stayed; or the plaintiff may refuse to accept the money in satisfaction, and reply accordingly, in which case the money shall remain in court, subject to the provisions hereinafter mentioned.

(*b*.) If the plaintiff accept the money so paid in he shall, after service of such notice in the Form No. 4 in Appendix B., as is in Rule 7 mentioned, or, after delivery of a reply accepting the money, be entitled to have the money paid out to himself on request, or to his solicitor, on the plaintiff's written authority, unless the court or judge shall otherwise order.

(*c*.) If the plaintiff does not accept, in satisfaction of the claim or cause of action in respect of which the payment into court has been made, the sum so paid in, but proceeds with the action in respect of such claim or cause of action, or any part thereof, the money shall remain in court and be subject to the order of the court or a judge, and shall not be paid out of court except in pursuance of an order. If the plaintiff proceeds with the action in respect of such claim or cause of action, or any part thereof, and recovers less than the amount paid into court, the amount paid in shall be applied, so far as is necessary, in satisfaction of the plaintiff's claim, and the balance (if any) shall, under such order, be repaid to the defendant. If the defendant succeeds in respect of such claim or cause of action, the whole amount shall, under such order, be repaid to him.

7. The plaintiff, when payment into court is made before delivery of defence may, within four days after the receipt of

notice of such payment, or when such payment is first signified
in a defence, may, before reply, accept in satisfaction of the claim
or cause of action in respect of which such payment has been
made, the sum so paid in, in which case he shall give notice to the
defendant in the Form No. 4 in Appendix B., and shall be at
liberty, in case the entire claim or cause of action is thereby
satisfied, to tax his costs after the expiration of four days from
the service of such notice, unless the court or a judge shall otherwise order, and, in case of non-payment of the costs within 48
hours after such taxation, to sign judgment for his costs so taxed.

[Form No. 4 referred to in the foregoing Rules 6 and 7[1]]

Take notice that the plaintiff accepts the sum of   *l.*
paid by you into court in satisfaction of the claim in respect of
which it is paid in.

THIRD SCHEDULE.

TABLE OF FEES.

Appointed by the Commissioners, with the concurrence of the Lord
Chancellor and of the Treasury, to be taken in relation to the proceedings before the Commissioners.

	£	s.	d.	
Receiving and filing every application or statement of case, or answer thereto,	1	0	0	Fees in ordinary cases.
Receiving and filing every reply, affidavit, or other proceeding,	0	2	6	
Note.—No extra charge is to be made for documents that may accompany any application, answer, reply, or affidavit.				
Every summons upon interlocutory proceedings,	0	5	0	Fees in ordinary cases.
Every order made thereon,	0	2	6	
Attendance by counsel on interlocutory proceedings, each side,	0	10	0	
For every appointment for hearing,	0	2	6	
Every subpœna,	0	2	6	
Every hearing not in the nature of an interlocutory proceeding, or of an arbitration,	1	0	0	
Office copy of proceedings, per folio,	0	0	6	
Note.- Copies of plans, sections, etc., to be paid for by the party requiring them according to the actual cost.				
Every commission to take evidence,	1	0	0	Fees on commissions.

[1] *See* note on page 106.

	£	s.	d.	
Every hearing in the nature of an arbitration between railway companies or canal companies, or between railway companies and the Postmaster-General under the Regulation of Railways Acts, 1873 and 1874, or either of them, each day or part of a day, ...	15	15	0	Fees on hearings in the nature of arbitrations.
Every decision of such difference, . . .	5	5	0	
Every hearing in the nature of an arbitration, one of the parties being other than a railway company or canal company, each day or part of a day, ...	5	5	0	
Every decision of such difference, . . .	2	2	0	
Note.—The fee for the hearing is to be paid on each day by the party whose case is then being heard, unless the Commissioners otherwise order.				

All fees shall be paid by stamps, impressed on the forms applicable to the various proceedings respectively, which shall be sold in London at the office of the Commissioners, West Front Committee Rooms, House of Lords, S.W.; and at the Inland Revenue Office, Somerset House; and at the Branch Office, Royal Courts of Justice. In Edinburgh, at the Inland Revenue Office, Waterloo Place. In Dublin, at the Inland Revenue Office, Custom House; and at such other places as the Inland Revenue Department may determine.

FOURTH SCHEDULE.

DIRECTIONS of the Railway and Canal Commissioners relating to working agreements between two or more railway companies.

1. Care should be taken that at least 28 days from the date of the newspaper containing the first insertion of the notice to the public, of the intention of the companies to enter into a working agreement, are allowed for bringing objections before the Railway and Canal Commissioners, and that during the whole of that period a copy of the proposed working agreement is lodged at the Commissioners' office for inspection.

2. At the expiration of the period specified in the notices for bringing objections before the Railway and Canal Commissioners, and together with the application for their approval, there should be sent to their office:

a. The Act or Acts of Parliament authorising such agreement.

b. Copies of the newspapers containing the notices of the intention of the two companies to enter into such agreement which are required by the 24th section of the Railway Clauses Act, 1863.

c. Copies of the newspapers containing the advertisements of each Company, required by the 23rd section of the same Act, convening the special meetings at which the agreement was assented to.

d. A copy of the circular which was addressed to each shareholder.

e. The agreement, sealed by the companies, together with a certificate given under the hands of the chairman at the meeting, and of the secretary of each company, stating that such agreement was duly assented to by the required proportion of the votes of the shareholders and stockholders entitled to vote in that behalf at meetings of the company, present (personally or by proxy) at a general meeting of each of the companies specially convened for that purpose, pursuant to the 23rd section of the same Act.

3. The application to the Commissioners for their approval should be made in the manner prescribed by their General Rules of February 1889, Nos. 2 and 6.

The agreement, when approved by the Commissioners, will be returned with their approval signified thereon, and the copy lodged at their office will be retained by them.

NOTE. *Where the special Act or Acts authorising the agreement do not incorporate the Railway Clauses Act, 1863, Part 3, or are of an earlier date, the course of proceeding will be that indicated in the special Acts.*

LIST OF CASES CITED

(IN SUPPLEMENT).

ABERDEEN Joint-station Committee and G. N. S. R. v. N. B. R., pp. 17, 18, 19.
Adams v. G. N. S. R., p. 51.
Aitken v. N. B. R., p. 27.
Anderson v. Glasgow Tramways Co., p. 27.
Att.-Gen. and Hare v. Met. R. C., p. 57.
Att.-Gen. v. St. John's Hospital, Bath, p. 62.

Barnett v. G. & S. W. R., p. 41.
Barr & Sons v. C. R., p. 17.
Barton v. L. & N. W. R., p. 68.
Becke v. Stratford-on-Avon R. C., p. 60.
Bell v. G. N. R. of I., p. 28.
Bentley v. M. S. & L. R. C., p. 58.
Bergheim v. S. E. R., p. 25.
Birmingham and Dist. Land Co. v. L. & N. W. R., p. 59.
Birmingham and Dist. Land Co. v. L. & N. W. R. (No. 2), p. 59.
Ex p. Bradford and District Tramways Co., p. 67.
In re The Brighton and Dyke R. C., p. 63.
In re Brooshooft's Settlement, p. 62.
Brotherton v. Metr. Dist. Joint Committee, p. 33.
Brown v. Eastern and Midland R. C., p. 41.
Budd v. L. & N. W. R., p. 5.
Burrup and Others v. L. & S. W. R., pp. 57, 67.
Byrne v. G. S. & W. R., p. 28.

Cairns v. C. R., p. 46.
C. R. v. Cross, p. 1.
C. R. v. M'Bride, p. 57.
Ex p. Chambers, p. 67.
City and South London R. C. v. London C. C., p. 56.

Clifford v. Imperial Brazilian R. C., p. 68.
Clogher Valley Tramway Co. v. The Queen, p. 49.
Cobb v. G. W. R., p. 30.
In re Colchester Tramways Co., p. 67.
Cole v. Miles, p. 43.
Conservators of Thames v. London, Tilbury, and Southend R. C., p. 58.
Consett Waterworks Co. v. Ritson, p. 36.
Coultas v. Victorian R. Comrs., pp. 28, 43.
Cowper Essex v. Local Board for Acton, p. 58.
Craig v. N. B. R., p. 31.
Cramb v. C. R., p. 44.
Crawford v. Portpatrick and Girvan Joint Committee, p. 21.
Curtin v. G. S. & W. R., p. 42.
Cusack v. L. & N. W. R., p. 26.
Cutbill v. Shropshire R. C., p. 67.

Dalmellington Iron Co. v. G. & S. W. R., p. 13.
Delaney v. Dublin United Tramways Co., p. 33.
Denaby Main Col. Co. v. M. S. & L. R. C., p. 5.
Dickson v. G. N. R., p. 7.
Donovan v. Laing, Wharton, and Down Cons. Synd., Lim., p. 47.
Dowling v. Pontypool, etc., R. C., p. 55.
Duke of Richmond and Gordon v. G. N. S. R., p. 38.
In re Dublin, Wicklow, and Wexford R. C., ex p. Jordan, p. 62.

Earl of Hopetoun v. N. B. R., p. 35.
In re the East London R. C., Oliver's Claim, p. 59.
East and West India Docks v. Shaw, Savill, & Albion Co., p. 4.
In re East and West India Dock Co., p. 63.
In re Eastern and Midlands R. C., p. 63.
In re Eastern and Midlands R. C. (2), p. 63.
In re Enniskillen and Bundoran R. C., p. 68.
Evershed v. L. & N. W. R., p. 5.

Finck v. L. & S. W. R., p. 54.
Flood v. C. R., p. 40.
Ford v. L. & S. W. R., p. 9.
Forfar and Brechin R. C. v. Bell, p. 52.
Forth Bridge R. C. v. Assessor for Queensferry, p. 65.

Gillespie v. Lucas & Aird, p. 39.
Gilmour v. N. B. R., p. 38.
Glasgow District Subway Co. v. Johnstone, p. 53.
Glasgow Subway Co. v. Provan, p. 57.
G. & S. W. R. v. Bain, p. 35.
Glover and Others, p. 61.
Grand Trunk R. of Canada v. Jennings, p. 43.
Gray v. N. B. R., p. 22.
G. N. R. v. Winder, p. 33.
G. W. R. v. Bunch, p. 25.
Groom v. G. W. R., p. 35.

Harris v. L. & S. W. R., p. 39.
Harris v. N. B. R., p. 32.
Harris v. Cockermouth, etc., R. C., p. 5.
Harrison & Camm v. M. R., p. 13.
Haughton v. N. B. R., p. 41.
Herron v. Rathmine Commissioners, p. 54.
H. R. v. G. N. S. R., p. 6.
  „   „   (1891), p. 7.
  „   „   (1890), p. 16.

In re Hull, Barnsley, and West Riding Junction R. C., p. 64.
H. R. v. Special Commissioners of Income-Tax, p. 66.
How v. L. & N. W. R., p. 22.
Hunt v. G. N. R., p. 48.
Hunt v. G. N. R. (2), p. 48.

Ivens v. G. W. R., p. 21.

Johnson v. Lindsay, p. 47.
Johnson v. N. E. R., p. 17.
Johnston v. C. R., p. 31.
Johnston v. G. N. R., p. 28.

Kehoe v. Waterford and Limerick R. C., p. 68.
Kelly v. Munster and Leinster Bank, p. 68.
Kennedy v. G. S. & W. R., p. 67.
Knights v. L. C. & D. R. C., p. 32.
Knowles v. L. & Y. R. C., p. 36.

Lamb v. G. N. R., p. 48.
Lambert v. Dublin, Wicklow, and Wexford R. C., p. 53.
L. & Y. R. C. v. Mayor of Bury, p. 43.
Liverpool Corn Trade Association v. G. W. R., pp. 5, 10.
" " v. L. & N. W. R., p. 10.
Lockyer v. Int. Sleeping Car Co., p. 31.
Logan Petitioner, p. 62.
L. B. & S. C. R. v. Watson, p. 33.
L. C. & D. R. C. v. S. E. R. C., p. 16.
L. C. & D. R. C. v. S. E. R. C., p. 65.
L. & N. W. R. v. Boulton, p. 59.
L. & N. W. R. v. Evans, p. 36.
L. & N. W. R. v. Hughes, p. 21.
London, Tilbury, and Southend R. C. v. Trs. of Gower's Walk Schools, p. 58.
Lord Advocate v. Forth Bridge R. C., p. 66.
Lowe v. G. N. R., p. 32.
Lowther v. C. R., p. 58.

M'Alpine v. Lanarkshire and Ayrshire R. C., p. 50.
Macandrew, Wright & Murray v. N. B. R., p. 62.
M'Callum v. N. B. R., p. 47.
M'Corkindale v. C. R., p. 53.
Macdonald v. H. R., p. 31.
M'Donnell v. G. S. & W. R., p. 47.
Macfarlane v. N. B. R., p. 6.
" v. G. N. S. R., p. 31.
M'Fee v. Police Commissioners of Broughty-Ferry, p. 40.
M'Gregor v. N. B. R., p. 55.
Mackinnon v. G. & S. W. R., p. 14.
M'Laren v. C. R., p. 39.
M'Laurin v. N. B. R., p. 30.
Magistrates of Elgin v. H. R., p. 53.
" of Glasgow v. C. R., p. 60.
" of Inverness v. H. R., p. 53.
Maidstone Town Council v. S. E. R. and L. C. & D. R. C., p. 7.
Main v. Lanarkshire and Dumbartonshire R. C., p. 34.
In re Manchester, Middleton, and District Tramway Co., p. 67.
M. S. & L. R. C. v. Assessment Committee of Doncaster Union, p. 67.
M. S. & L. R. C. v. North Central Waggon Co., p. 17.
" v. Sheffield and South Yorkshire Navigation Co., p. 56.

LIST OF CASES CITED

Marquis of Salisbury *v.* L. & N. W. R., p. 58.
Membery *v.* G. W. R., p. 46.
Metropolitan District R. C. *v.* Metropolitan R. C., p. 68.
Metropolitan R. C. *v.* Fowler, p. 66.
Middlemass *v.* N. B. R., p. 31.
M. R. *v.* Martin & Co., p. 21.
M. R. C. *v.* Robinson, p. 36.
Morris *v.* Tottenham and Forest Gate R. C., p. 61.
Muir *v.* C. R., p. 60.
Myers *v.* Catterson, p. 39.

In re Neath and Brecon R. C., 63.
Nevin & Farrell *v.* G. S. & W. R. C., p. 24.
Newman *v.* L. & S. W. R., p. 42.
Newry Navigation Co. *v.* G. N. of I. R. C., p. 8.
Noble *v.* Killick, p. 33.
N. B. R. *v.* Garroway, pp. 14, 17, 19, 20.
   ,, *v.* Mackintosh, p. 45.
   ,, *v.* Magistrates of Edinburgh, p. 55.
   ,, *v.* Moore, p. 38.
   ,, *v.* Russell, p. 2.
   ,, *v.* Whyte, p. 38.
   ,, *v.* Wood, p. 30.
North Lonsdale Iron and Steel Co. *v.* Furness R. C., p. 9.
N. E. R. *v.* Kingston-upon-Hull, p. 16.
   ,, *v.* Reg., p. 49.
Nicholls *v.* N. E. R., p. 20.
Nisbet-Hamilton *v.* N. B. R., 35.
The Nizam State R. *v.* Wyatt, p. 67.

O'Gorman *v.* Sweet, p. 45.
Overseers of Putney *v.* L. & S. W. R., p. 57.

Palmer *v.* C. R., p. 65.
Pelsall Coal and Iron Co. *v.* L. & N. W. R., p. 11.
Pelsall Coal and Iron Co. *v.* L. & N. W. R. (No. 2), p. 11.
Ex p. Perpetual Curate of Bilston, p. 62.
Pickering Phipps *v.* L. & N. W. R., pp. 5, 10.
Pirie *v.* C. R., p. 26.
Pope *v.* M. & S. W. J. R. C., p. 68.
Port-Glasgow and Newark Sailcloth Co. *v.* C. R., p. 35.

Portway v. Colne Valley and Halstead R. C., pp. 12, 34.
Pounder v. N. E. R., p. 29.
Proffitt v. The Wye R. C., p. 64.
Protheroe v. Tottenham and Forest Gate R. C., p. 55.

Queen v. Distington Iron Co., p. 3.

Ray v. Walker, p. 56.
Rayson v. South London Tramways Co., p. 33.
Reg. v. G. W. R. ex p. the Ruabon B. & T.-C. Co., p. 37.
Reg. v. Schofield, p. 42.
Rhymney R. C. v. Rhymney Iron Co., p. 3.
Robinson v. John Watson, Lim., pp. 17, 47.
Roche v. Cork, Blackrock, and Passage R. C., p. 26.
Roe v. G. & S. W. R., p. 27.
Rohl v. Metr. R. C., p. 27.
Ruabon Brick and Terra-Cotta Co. v. G. W. R., p. 36.
Ryan v. G. S. W. R., p. 34.

Sadler v. S. Staffordshire and Birmingham Dist. Street Tramways Co., pp. 17, 42.
Sheridan v. M. G. W. R., p. 23.
Silver v. G. N. S. R., p. 31.
Skipwith v. G. W. R., p. 25.
Smith v. Baker & Sons, p. 46.
Smith v. H. R., p. 40.
In re Smith ex p. L. & N. W. R. and M. R., p. 62.
S. E. R. C. v. Corp. of Hastings, p. 7.
Sowerby v. G. N. R., p. 4.
Stewart v. H. R., p. 52.
Stirling-Stuart v. C. R., p. 61.

Taff Vale R. C., pp. 5, 17.
Taff Vale R. C. v. Barry Docks and Railway Co., p. 5.
Taff Vale v. Barry Docks and Railway Co. (No. 1), p. 12.
Taylor & Co. v. G. & S. W. R., p. 14.
In re Thackwray's and Young's Contract, p. 56.
Thatcher v. G. W. R., p. 41.
Tomlinson v. L. & N. W. R., p. 12.
Town Comrs. of Newry v. G. N. of I. R. C., p. 8.
Town Council of Oban v. Callander and Oban R. C., p. 52.
In re Uxbridge and Rickmansworth R. C., p. 67.

Victorian R. Comrs. v. Coultas, pp. 28, 43.

Walker v. G. N. R. of I., p. 28.
Watson v. N. B. R., p. 17.
Webb v. Shropshire R. C., p. 68.
Wentworth v. Hull & N. W. J. R. C., p. 56.
West v. L. & W. R., p. 4.
In re The West Lancashire R. C., p. 63.
Wharton v. L. & Y. R. C., p. 28.
Wilson v. C. R., p. 65.
Winsford Local Board v. Cheshire Lines Committee, p. 7.
Wood v. N. B. R., p. 28.

Yeats Trs. v. G. & S. W. R., p. 2.
Young v. S. E. R. C., p. 33.

INDEX.

Access to competing lines, 5.
Accident—
  Alleged acts of negligence, 42.
  At level crossing, 42, 43.
  Defective points, 42.
  Child killed on private harbour line, 39, 40.
  Co. exercising running powers, 12.
  Contributory negligence, 26, 27.
  Door not fastened, 31.
  Duty to warn, 27.
  Facilities for alighting, 28.
  Failure to light station, 26.
  Fault of servant outwith employment, 27.
  Head out of window, 26, 27.
  Heap left beside road, 41.
  Infant injured *en route sa mère*, 28.
  Injury from fright only, 28, 43.
  Leaving train in motion, 26.
  New trial twice granted, 40.
  Person lawfully on platform, 41.
  Precaution for servants, 46.
  Railway near docks, 41.
  Reasonable facility for public purpose, 26.
  Reasonable precaution, 41.
  Special duty to children, 40, 41.
  Death of stepmother, 28.
  Temporary control by others, 27.
  To contractor's servant, 46.
  To servant of adjoining proprietor, 40.
  To stationmaster, 46, 47.
  To surfaceman, 46.
  Underline bridge, 40.
"Accommodation, Conveniences, and Facilities," 6.
Accommodation Works, 34.

Act of 1845, sect. 16, 39.
,, 1845, sects. 61 & 150, 34.
,, 1845, sect. 70, 35.
,, 1845, sect. 71, 36.
,, 1845, sect. 83, 1, 2, 3.
,, 1845, "Injuriously affected," 57.
,, 1845 (reasonable suspicion of offence against), 33.
,, 1845 (Eng.), 5.
,, 1845 (Eng.), sect. 15, 53.
,, 1845 (Eng.), sect. 16, 58.
,, 1845 (Eng.), sect. 32, 60.
,, 1845 (Eng.), sects. 46, 47, 61, & 62, 42.
,, 1845 (Eng.), sects. 68-73, 34.
,, 1845 (Eng.), sect. 76, 12.
,, 1845 (Eng.), sects. 77, 78, & 79, 36.
,, 1845 (Eng.), sects. 3, 86, & 92, 12.
,, 1845 (Eng.), sect. 138, 64.
,, 1854, sect. 2, 5.
,, 1854, sect. 2, 7, 8, 9.
,, 1854, sects. 2 & 3, 1, 3.
,, 1854, sects. 1, 2, & 3, 7.
,, 1854, sect. 7, 22.
,, 1873, 3.
,, 1873, sect. 6, 1, 83.
,, 1873, sect. 8, 83.
,, 1873, sect. 9, 84.
,, 1873, sect. 10, 84.
,, 1873, sect. 14, 10, 11, 83, 84.
,, 1873, sect. 15, 4, 85.
,, 1873, sect. 16, 85.
,, 1873, sect. 17, 85.
,, 1873, sect. 19, 87.
,, 1874, 87.
,, 1888, 2.
,, 1888, sects. 1 & 8, 7.

INDEX

Act of 1888, sect. 2, 12.
,, 1888, sect. 7, 83.
,, 1888, sects. 7 & 14, 7.
,, 1888, sects. 7 & 27, 9.
,, 1888, sect. 9, 83.
,, 1888, sect. 10, 4, 85.
,, 1888, sects. 12 & 58, 1.
,, 1888, sects. 14, 33, & 34, 10, 11.
,, 1888, sects. 17, 27, 29-55, 5.
,, 1888, sects. 20, 86.
,, 1888, sect. 25, 84.
,, 1888, sect. 27, 5.
,, 1888, sect. 29, 9.
,, 1888, sects. 33 & 34, 83, 84.
,, 1888, sect. 37, 85.
,, 1888, sect. 38, 86.
,, 1889, 33, 69.
,, 1889, sect. 5, 32, 33.
,, 1889, sect. 7, 45.
,, Sederunt (1889) as to procedure in R. & C. T. Appeals, 80, 81.
Adjoining Proprietors, 34-39.
Adjournment (R. & C. Com. Court), 99.
Affidavits, 97.
Alteration of order (R. & C. Com.), 96.
Alternative rate, 22, 23.
Alternative routes, 15.
Amendment, 99.
Answer in R. & C. Com. Court, 89.
Answer (form of), 103.
Appeal from Sheriff, 57.
Appeal to Sheriff re accommodation works, 34.
Appeals under Railway and Canal Traffic Act, 1888, procedure in, 80, 81.
Application, form of, 102.
Application to R. & C. Commission, 83-87.
Appointing hearing (R. & C. Com. Court), 94.
Approaches to stations, 72.
Arbitration, 49, 50, 51, 64, 65.
Assessment, deficiencies in, 57.
Authority of Company's servants to remove, 32.
Avoiding payment of fare, 71.

Block system, 69.

Board of Trade, powers of, as to hours of work, 75.
Booking office, 7.
Booking to stations off line, 10.
Brakes (continuous), 70.
Branch railway, 11.
Branch railway (severing connection), 12.
Branch railways, 34.
Bridges, maintenance of, 43.
Building agreement, 59.
Buildings—erection beyond street line, 55, 56.

Carcass, sale of, 24.
Carriage, 17.
Carriage of goods, 20, 21.
Carriage of live-stock, 21-24.
Carriage of passengers, 26-35.
Carriage—liability for contamination of food, 43, 44.
Carrier, 8.
Charge for haulage, 12.
Charges disproportionate to distance, 8.
Charges, right to sell goods to defray warehouse, 21.
Cheap Trains Act, 1883, 87.
Clerical work, servant engaged in 76.
Cloak-room, bag left in, 25.
Close of pleadings, 90.
Common employment, 47.
Companies Clauses Act (Eng.), 1845, sect. 18, 68; sect. 65, 67; sect. 135, 64.
Compensation, 51, 57-59.
Compensation, failure of statutory tribunal, 58.
Compensation, mode of assessing, 59.
Compensation, principles of assessing, 58.
Compulsory powers, 51, 52, 53, 55, 56, 60.
Computation of time, 98.
Condition on left-luggage ticket, 25.
Condition precedent, 5.
Condition restricting liability absent, 25.
Confirmation of scheme, 63.
Consent cases, 89.

Consigned compensation, 61, 62.
Continuous brakes, 70.
Continuous line of communication, 7.
Contractors for works, 49, 51.
Conveniences, 6.
Conveyance, 17.
Conveyance (not statutory), 55.
Conveyance of Mails Act, 1893, 49, 77.
Conveyance of Mails Act, 1893 (text), 77-80.
Costs, 11, 12.
Covenant to re-sell, 56.

Damage —
  Caused by working of railway, 34, 35.
  Want of care in dangerous operations, 39.
  Remoteness of, 28.
Damages —
  30, 31.
  Deduction for insurance, 43.
  Excess of, 30, 31.
  Reduced, 31.
  Remoteness of, 30, 43.
  How claimed before Commission, 87.
  Reference, whether claim excluded, 49.
"Dealing," 16.
Debenture-holders, 64.
Debenture stock (issue under Act of 1889), 70.
Debentures, interest on, 68.
Debentures, issue at discount, 68.
Defence to action for charges, 1.
Deficiency in rates, 57.
Delay of goods, 20.
"Delineated" on deposited plans, 54, 55.
Deposited Plans, 54.
Detain passenger, right to, 32.
Detain train, refusal to, on complaint, 29.
Detain waggons, right to, 17.
Detention of goods, 21.
Detention of trains, 31.
Deviation, lateral and vertical, 54.
Deviation, limits of, 53.

Difference as to renumeration for conveyance of mails, 77.
Differences under Conveyance of Mails Act, 1893, 79.
Diligence, 19.
Diligence, business books, income-tax receipts, report by station-master, 31.
Diligence, writings passing between Company and contractor, 39.
Discharge of claim for damages, 30.
Discovery of documents, 92.
Dismissal, publication of, 48.
Disqualification of arbiter, 50.
Dividend out of capital, 68.
Documents, diligence and production in R. & C. Com. Court, 92, 93.
Embankment, how valued, 65.
Engine, fires caused by, 34, 35.
Entry on lands taken, 53.
Excess fare, demand for, 33.
Excess luggage, 26.
Excess of damages, 30, 31.
Excess in arbiter's award, 50.
Excessive charges, 3.
Excessive hours, 75.
Expenses in connection with consigned money, 61, 62.
Extension constituted separate undertaking, 62.
Extension of time clause in contract, 50.
Evidence (in R. & C. Com. Court), 95.

Facilities, 3, 5, 6, 7.
Facilities, reasonable, in forwarding goods, 20.
Facilities (resumption of passenger traffic), 7.
Facility for public purpose, 26.
Fare, action to recover, 32, 33.
Fares and tickets, 31, 33.
Fees (before R. & C. Com.), 101.
Fence, duty to, 34.
Fence, sufficiency of, 34.
Ferry, right to exclude public, 44.
Feu-charter and Special Act, 55.
Filing application, 88.
Formal objections, 90.

INDEX

Forms (R. & C. Com. proceedings), 101-106.
Forwarding of goods, 20.
"Fronts or abuts," 57.

"General purposes" rate, 57, 67.
Government guarantee, 68.
Gross traffic receipts, 64.
Group rates, 9.
Guard not a "workman" in sense of Truck Acts, 47, 48.
Guard and porter, Truck Acts, 48.

Haulage contract, 16.
Haulage of waggons, 12.
Hearing (R. & C. Com. Court), 94.
"Hereditament," 66.
Hours of labour, 75.

Income-tax, 65, 66, 67.
Increased cost of working, 8.
Indorsement (form of), 102.
Indorsement on application, 88.
Indorsement (Rule 4) (form of), 103.
"Injuriously affected," 57, 58.
Inquiry by Board of Trade into hours worked, 75.
Interdict, 55.
Interdict against careless conduct of work under statutory powers, 39.
Interest, claim for, under traffic agreement, 16.
Interest in land, 59.
Interest of public, 9.
Interim injunction, 91.
Interlocking of points and signals, 70.
Interlocutory applications, 96.
Interpretation (R. & C. Com. Rules), 82.
Invalid chair, 26.
Issues (in R. & C. Com. Court), 90.
Joint-committee, 18.
Joint-owner (of station), 18.
Joint-station, right to use under running powers, 19.
Joint-station, title to sue, 18.
Joint traffic agreement, 16.
Judgment (R. & C. Com. Court), 95.
Jurisdiction, 64, 65.
Jurisdiction of R. & C. Com., 3.

Land tax, 66.
Lands Clauses Acts—
  1845, 62.
  1845, sects. 17 & 115, 51.
  1845, sects. 17, 83, 87 ; 112, 114, 53.
  1845, sects. 67 & 79, 61, 62.
  1845, sects. 80, 107, etc., 117 & 126, 53.
  1845, sect. 120, 52.
  1845, sect. 126, 53.
  1845, sect. 139, 57.
  1845 (Eng.), sect. 16, 56.
  1845 (Eng.), sect. 133, 57.
Level crossing at station, duty to warn, 43.
Level crossing, power of justices to order handrails, etc., 42.
Level crossings, 42, 43.
Libel, publication of offenders' names, 48.
Line, liability to reinstate, 37.
Line partly in England, service, 64.
Live stock, custody of, 21.
Live stock, damages where joint fault, 22.
Live stock, escape of dog, responsibility for injuries caused by, 22.
Lower charge in public interest, 9.
"Loss," 25.
"Lower rates," 13.
Lower rates or tolls, 5.

Mails, conditions when carried on tramways, 77, 78.
"Mails," definition of, 79.
Maintenance of bridges, 43.
Merchandise traffic, facilities for, 7.
Minerals—
  Freestone, 35.
  Limestone, 36.
  Line coming down in consequence of working, 37.
  Notice, 36.
  Open workings, 36, 37.
  Right to work under line, 36, 37.
  Shale in banks of cutting, 35.
  In vicinity, 35-37.
Misdelivery, 25.
"Most favoured trader" clause, 13.
Municipal authority, consent of, 55.

I

"Necessary and convenient for traffic," 39.
Necessary purpose, 60.
Negligence (carriage of live stock), 23.
Notice (Rule 11), (form of), 105.
Notice of discontinuance, 94.
Notice to admit, 93.
Notice to produce, 93.
Notice to public of agreements (form of), 105.
Notice to take, 51.

Obligation to build up side arches of river bridge, 38.
Obstruction on railway, 45.
Office of registrar (R. & C. Com.), 98.
Option to purchase, time in which to be exercised, 56.
Order to distinguish, 11.
Order to divide, 10.
"Ordinary trains," 38.
Overcharges, 1, 2, 3, 13.
Overcrowding of carriage, 29.
Overtime, returns of, 71.

Parcels, delivery of, 8.
Parliamentary deposit, 67, 68.
Passenger—
 Arrest for refusal to show ticket, 33.
 Duty to, violence of fellow-passengers, 29.
 Giving false name or address, 33, 71.
 Provisions as to fares and tickets (Act of 1889), 71.
 Refusal to pay fare, 33.
 Right to detain, 32.
 Right to remove, 31, 32.
 Robbery of, 29.
 Travelling without payment of fare, 33.
 Under influence of drink, 33.
 Using ticket for wrong station, 32, 33.
Passenger station, merchandise traffic at, 8.
Passenger traffic, facilities for, 7.
Passenger traffic, order to resume, 7.
Passengers, accidents to, 26-36.

Passengers, carriage of, 26-35.
Passengers' luggage, 25, 26.
Payment for accommodation, etc., 6.
Payment into Court, 106-108.
Penalties for entry, 53.
Penalties for failure to give returns of overtime, 71.
Permanent improvements, 65.
"Person interested," 10.
Pleadings by leave, 90.
Poisoning caused by contamination of goods in carriage, 43, 44.
Post Office—
 Misappropriation of money belonging to, 49.
 Special control of railway servants by, 27.
Parcels Act, 1882, 49, 77.
Practice (of Superior Courts), when applicable to R. & C. Com. proceedings, 99, 100.
Preferential dock dues, 3.
Preliminary communication, 91.
Preliminary meeting, 91.
Preliminary questions, 91.
Private engine, 17.
Private waggons, 16, 17.
Procedure before Railway Commission, 6, 82-110.
Procedure in Scotland, 6.
Procedure in Scotch appeals under Act of 1888, 80, 81.
Procedure, service, Scotch Company in England, 64.
Production of documents, 19.
Production of documents (R. & C. Com. Court), 93.
Prohibition, 3.
Promotion expenses, 67.
Public body, powers of, 73, 74.

Railway Commission—
 Cases appealed from, 4, 5.
 Cases before, 6-13.
 Procedure in Scotland, 6.
 Differences as to mails to be referred to, 77.
 Can enforce orders of Board of Trade under Act of 1889, 70.
 Powers of as to hours of labour, 76.

Railway and Canal Commission Rules, 82-110.
Railway and Canal Traffic (Provisional Orders), Amendment Act, 1891, 73.
Railway and Canal Traffic Act, 1892, 74.
Railway Companies Act, 1867, 62, 63, 64.
Railway Regulation Act, 1893, 48, 75.
Railway servants, hours of, 75.
Railway stock, certificate of, 68.
Rate-books, production of, 19.
Rates, 1, 2, 3, 13, 14.
    Order to divide in rate-book, 10.
    Order to distinguish, 11.
    For excess luggage, 26.
    For live stock, 24.
    "Rates in force and from time to time exacted," 14.
Rates under agreement, 11.
Rating, liability for river formed into canal, 67.
Reasonable conditions (carriage of live stock), 22, 23.
Receipts, 15.
Reconvey, obligation in favour of adjoining proprietor, 39.
Reference, specific and general, 15.
Registrar's office, 98.
Regulation of Railways Act, 1889, 32, 33, 45, 69.
Regulation of Railways Act, 1889 (text), 69.
Removal of passenger, 31, 32.
Repayment of deposit, 67.
Repetition of overcharges, 13.
Reply (in R. & C. Com. Court), 90.
Reply (form of), 104.
Rescission of order (R. & C. Com. Court), 96.
Right to detain live stock, 24.
Right-of-way, 43.
Roads and streets, interference with, 59, 60.
Robbery of passenger, 29.
Rolling stock, discretion to replace, 68.
"Route," 14.

Running powers, 5, 14, 17.
Running powers, liability of Co. exercising, for accidents, 42.

Safety of public, provisions for, 69, 70.
"Same portion of the line of railway," 2.
Sanitary rate, 67.
Schedule of time for duty of servants, 75.
Schemes of management—
    Non-assent of class, 63.
    Rights prejudicially affected, 63.
    Sale of undertaking, 63.
    Petition to sanction, 63.
Separate undertaking, 62.
Servants—
    Accidents to, 46, 47.
    Common employment, 47.
    Publication to, 48.
    In sense of Truck Acts, 47, 48.
Set-off of overcharges, 3.
Service of application (in R. & C. Com. Court), 88.
"Services incidental to the business of a carrier," 4.
Servitude, 55.
Servitude in land taken, 52.
Sittings of R. & C. Com., 98.
Sleeping-Car Co., 31.
Spark-arrester, 34, 35.
Special contract (carriage of live stock), 22, 23.
Special obligations, 37-39.
Specific implement, 38.
Station, 11.
Station, "temporary or permanent," 37.
Station accommodation, 4.
Stations, power to make bye-laws regulating use of, 45, 72.
Stationmaster—
    Accident to, 46.
    Authority of, to bind Company, 22.
    Land used as garden by, 39.
    Report by, 31.
Steam tramway, 49.
Streets, level interfered with, 59.
Streets, power to stop up: reference to arbiter, 60.

Subpœna (forms of), 104.
Substituted road, default in making, 60.
"Superfluous land," 52, 56.
Superior r. vassal, 53.
Surplus land, house thereon, obligation as to light, 39.
Suspension of proceedings before Commission, 89.

Table of fees (R. & C. Com. Court), 101, 108, 109.
"Taken for the purposes of the work," 57.
Taxation, 65, 66, 67.
Taxation of costs (R. & C. Com. Court), 96.
Telegraph Act, 1878, 87.
Temporary possession of land, 60.
Tenant's interest in land, 51.
Terminal charges, 4.
Ticket used for wrong station, 32, 33.
Tickets, questions as to, 31-33.
Tickets to have fare printed on, 72.
Time
  Abridgement of, 100.
  Enlargement of, 100.
  How computed, 98.
Title to land taken, 53.
Trader's waggons, 16, 17.
"Traders," 14.
Traffic questions, documents called for, 19.
Trains, obligation to stop, 37, 38.
Trains, "ordinary," 38.
"Tram road," definition of, 79.
Tram roads, mails on, 79.
"Tramway," definition of, 79.
Tramways, mails on, 77.

Transference of action, 1.
Transmission of documents and fees by post, 100.
Transmission of shares on death, 68.
Travelling without payment of fare, 71.
Trespass, powers of dealing with, 45.
Trespass on railway, 43.
Truck Acts, 47, 48.
Tunnel, liability for assessment, 66.

Undue preference, 1, 2, 3, 5, 8, 9, 13.
Undue preference of towns, 8.
Unfinished railway, 65.

Valuation, 65, 66, 67.
Ventilating shaft, construction of, 38.
Ventilator for underground station, 57.
View, 95.

Wages, written contract for deduction, 48.
Waggons, 12, 16, 17.
Waggons belonging to third party, right to detain, 17.
Warehouse charges, 21.
Warranty of punctuality, 31.
Widening of line, 53.
Witnesses (in R. & C. Com. Court), 94.
Witnesses in England, 31.
Whistle, omission to, 46, 47.
Working agreements, directions as to, 109, 110.
Working expenses, 62, 64.
Working of railway, damage caused by, 34, 35.
Works, abandonment of, 61, 67, 68.
Works, construction of, 60.
Workshops, servant engaged in, 76.

Printed by T. and A. CONSTABLE, Printers to Her Majesty,
at the Edinburgh University Press.

www.ingramcontent.com/pod-product-compliance
Lightning Source LLC
Chambersburg PA
CBHW022135160426
43197CB00009B/1291